Mark's Sketchbook of Christ

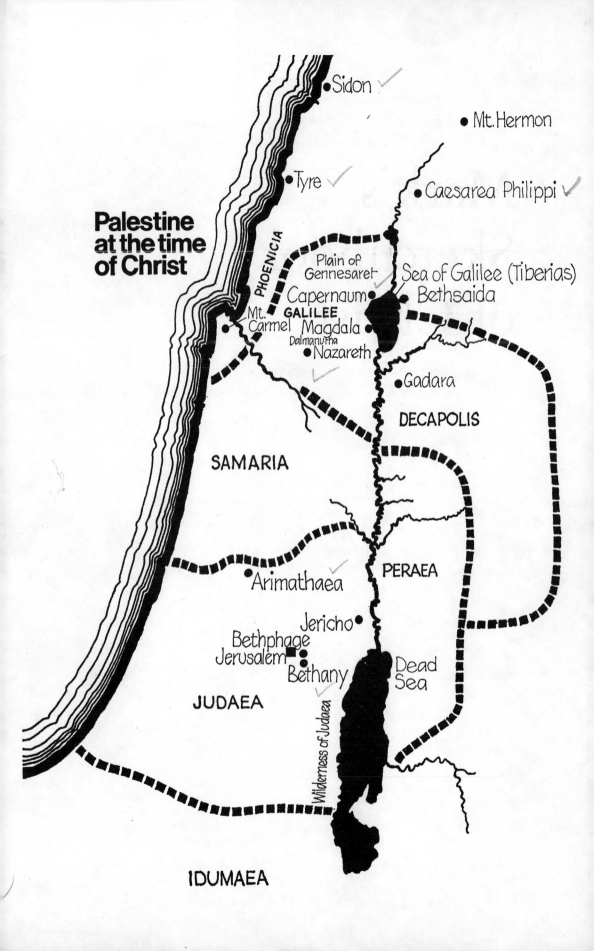

Palestine at the time of Christptem

Mark's Sketchbook of Christ

Helen J. Tenney

THE BANNER OF TRUTH TRUST

THE BANNER OF TRUTH TRUST
3 Murrayfield Road, Edinburgh, EH12 6EL
P.O. Box 621, Carlisle, Pennsylvania 17013, USA

© *Copyright 1956*
WM B. EERDMANNS PUBLISHING COMPANY
GRAND RAPIDS, MICHIGAN, USA

First Banner of Truth Trust edition 1971
Reprinted 1975
Reprinted 1978
Reprinted 1987

ISBN 0 85151 075 2

Printed in Great Britain by
Hazell Watson & Viney Limited
Member of BPCC plc
Aylesbury Bucks

To our sons Robert and Philip who
represent countless other young people
who need to study the Word of God
for themselves

Preface

Personal Bible study is more rewarding than any other. But how does one with little or no Biblical background get started? Or, how can the sincere but untrained teacher lead his pupils into the satisfying experience of discovering for themselves what the Word of God says?

These two questions and the needs of two teen-age sons in Christian schools kept pressing the author for an answer. The present Bible study workbook, combining the best features of the inductive method with an integrated outline, seemed the most satisfactory solution.

The Gospel of Mark was selected because of its adaptability to this method and because of its appeal to young people. This story of the life of Christ, though incomplete in some details, is fast moving, is picturesque in language, and gives a greater emphasis on His deeds than on His teachings. This Gospel provides a simple framework of events upon which more detailed study may be built later.

It is hoped that the method of Bible study provided in this workbook will prove useful in Bible courses in schools, in week-day church programmes, in summer camps, in vacation Bible school curricula, and on the foreign mission field.

Thanks are due to Mr P. B. Christie of Christian Publications, Harrisburg, Pa, for permission to reuse material first prepared for Sunday school lessons on the Gospel of Mark; to Miss Vivienne Blomquist, Chairman of the Department of Christian Education at Wheaton College, for reading the manuscript and offering helpful suggestions; and to the author's husband, Dr Merrill C. Tenney, Dean of the Graduate School of Wheaton College, for constant encouragement to commit to writing an idea.

Wheaton, Illinois   HJT
1956

Contents

Preface   vii

Introduction   xi

The author of the Gospel of Mark   xiii

1 *Beginnings* [1:1-45]   1

2 *Questions and answers* [2:1-3:6]   10

3 *Friends and foes* [3:7-35]   17

4 *Parables* [4:1-34]   21

5 *Miracles* [4:35-5:43]   26

6 *Opinions – pro and con* [6:1-56]   32

7 *Opposition – traditions* [7:1-37]   38

8 *Peter's confession* [8:1-38]   42

9 *Transfiguration* [9:1-50]   47

10 *Interviews* [10:1-52]   53

11 *Authority* [11:1-12:12]   60

12 *A day of questions* [12:13-44]   67

13 *The future* [13:1-37]   74

14 *Facing death* [14:1-72]   80

15 *Crucifixion* [15:1-47]   90

16 *Resurrection* [16:1-20]   95

Tips for teachers   99

Outlines of the Gospel of Mark   101

Special projects   102

Glossary   103

Notes   105

Maps

Palestine at the time of Christ (1)   ii

The Temple of Herod   73

Jerusalem   86

Palestine at the time of Christ (2)   98

Introduction

Just as the lightning chalk artist draws in quick bold lines, so the author of the Gospel of Mark sketches the life of Jesus Christ. The artist may use varied colours of chalk, short and long strokes, fine and broad lines, often concealing the design almost until the drawing is complete. When the last touch has been added, and the special lights have been turned on, the picture emerges in breath-taking beauty.

The Gospel of Mark is a series of scenes from the life of Christ, and tells more of what He did than what He taught. The scenes are sketched rapidly one after another, presenting Him as the great miracle worker as well as the great teacher. Anyone enlightened by the Holy Spirit, who reads this account of Jesus' life and deeds, will be driven to the conclusion of the Roman centurion at the cross: 'Truly this man was the Son of God' [15:39].

Using this workbook

A workbook automatically suggests questions and answers, fill-ins, or true and false questions. This workbook is different. The fill-ins are to be taken directly from Mark's Gospel and will fit around an outline.

If an assignment covers one chapter in Mark, read that complete chapter. Note how the chapter is divided into paragraphs or topics in the outline. Then, re-read one paragraph at a time in Mark before filling in the blanks in the workbook. Sometimes you will be searching for answers to questions; at other times you will simply fill in from the Bible text the explanation of the points in the outline. Whether you quote word for word or summarize, in general you may judge the length of the answer by the amount of space indicated for the fill-ins.

For example, on page 2:

John's habits of living

(1) Clothing ..... *camel's hair clothes, girdle of skin* .....

(2) Food ..... *locusts and wild honey* .....

Write neatly and legibly

ALWAYS READ DIRECTIONS CAREFULLY

The author of the Gospel of Mark

Look up these references, which are not here given in the order that you will need to use them, and insert the right references in the correct spaces below. Some may be used more than once. Colossians 4:10, 11; Acts 15:37, 38, 39; 9:27; 13:13; 13:5; 4:36, 37; 12:12; 12:25; Mark 14:51, 52; 2 Timothy 4:11; I Peter 5:13.

No mention of the author is made in the Gospel, but it is generally believed to be John Mark. He was the son of a certain Mary, probably a well-to-do widow residing in Jerusalem. It may have been in her home where Jesus kept the Passover with His disciples on the night of the betrayal. If so, it is possible that Mark was personally acquainted with Jesus and many of His followers, and may have witnessed some of the events of His life. Tradition points to him as 'the young man' [   ] who followed along in the curious mob at Jesus' betrayal, but who fled when He was arrested.

Mark had the advantage of a hospitable Christian home, where the twelve apostles and others of the Jerusalem church met frequently. To this home came Peter after his miraculous deliverance from prison [   ] and found a group of Christians praying for his release.

Mark was the cousin of Barnabas [   ], a wealthy landowner of Cyprus [   ], who accompanied Paul on his first missionary tour. When Barnabas and Paul returned from Jerusalem to Antioch, they took John Mark along with them [   ]. They shortly set out on their first missionary tour, with Mark added to their party as attendant or assistant [

]. At Perga in Pamphylia Mark deserted and returned to Jerusalem

[   ]. Perhaps he was homesick or could not stand the hardships of the journey. Whatever the reason, cousin Barnabas wanted to give him a second opportunity of service, but Paul was unwilling to risk another desertion [

].

This disagreement led Paul and Barnabas into separate ministries. Kind-hearted Barnabas, who had once befriended Paul [   ], now took his young relative to help with missionary work in Cyprus [   ].

Later the breach between Paul and Mark was healed. Writing from his prison in Rome to the Colossian Christians, Paul stated that Mark was a comfort to him [   ]. During his second imprisonment, Paul instructed Timothy to bring Mark to Rome, saying, 'for he is profitable to me for the ministry' [   ]. Without a doubt Mark had grown more courageous and successfully faced the responsibilities of leadership in the early Christian church.

Mark continued to be also the friend and associate of Peter from his youth to Peter's last imprisonment. In fact, Peter referred to him in one of his epistles as 'Marcus my son' [   ]. It is generally believed that Mark received most of the facts of the gospel story from Peter whose vivid memory retained the smallest details of his Master's life.

KEY VERSE: *Mark* 10:45

Mark presents Jesus as the busy Servant. Memorize Mark 10:45: 'For even the Son of man came not to be ministered unto, but to minister, and to give his life a ransom for many.'

1 Beginnings

[1:1-45]

Title

The opening words of the Gospel of Mark give its title: 'The beginning of the gospel of Jesus Christ, the Son of God' [1:1]. Without any reference to the birth or early life of Jesus, the author points directly to the beginning of His public ministry and the spreading of the *good news* concerning Him.

The gospel is a Person – 'Jesus Christ, the Son of God.' When it was announced that Mary would have a son, the angel said, 'Thou shalt call his name JESUS: for he shall save his people from their sins' [Matt 1:21]. The name Jesus, then, marked Him as a human being and was the name by which He was known in His family and through all subsequent history.

'Christ' [the anointed One: see Acts 10:38] was an official title which signified that Jesus had a special appointment from God for a special task. It was the same as the Old Testament term *Messiah* and pointed to Jesus as the fulfilment of all the prophecies that promised a Messiah and a Deliverer for the Jews.

The phrase, 'Son of God,' showed that Jesus was divine as well as human. His authority and power came from God, who was His Father. At the early age of twelve years, He realized how important His life and work would be. When His worried parents found Him in the temple after a frantic three-day search, He said in a matter-of-fact way, 'Wist ye not that I must be about my Father's business?' [Luke 2:49].

Preparation for the Gospel 1:2-13

By the prophets 1:2, 3

Arrange in the parallel columns below the prophecies and Mark's statement of their fulfilment.

MALACHI 3:1	MARK 1:2
....	....
....	....
....	....
....	....
....	....

....

....

....

....

....

These two prophecies speak of a *messenger* and a *message* which would prepare the way for the coming of the Son of God. The figure of speech used is taken from the custom of sending an officer before a king about to make a royal journey, to smooth and repair the highways to guarantee a safe trip. The messenger was also a herald – like the town crier of bygone days – to announce the coming of the monarch.

Thus, Mark focuses attention on the centuries-old predictions to declare, 'This *voice* was John the Baptist.' John identified himself with the voice in the wilderness [John 1:23], and Jesus confirmed it [Matt 11:7-14].

By John the Baptist 1:4-8

John's methods [4]

(1) ....

(2) ....

John's success [5] ....

....

John's habits of living [6]

(1) Clothing ....

(2) Food ....

John's humility [7, 8]

(1) ....

(2) ....

[To undo the 'shoe latchet' was the duty of a slave.]
[2]

For a more complete background of the life of John the Baptist, read Luke 1:5-25, 57-80, especially verses 76-80. Although the son of the priest Zacharias, and probably well educated, John spent most of his early manhood 'in the wilderness' – a wild region around the Jordan river. There he lived a stern and disciplined life because of his devotion to God. His clothing and food were products of the barren countryside. His preaching was intended to arouse the Jews from their dead formal worship and to announce a new Deliverer, who would be *the Messiah*. He called upon men to repent.

By John's baptism of Jesus 1:9-11 [Parallel passages, Matt 3:13-17, Luke 3:21-23]

Jesus came from...
This was the home city of Joseph and Mary [Luke 2:39].

List the three events which accompanied Jesus' baptism by John.

(1) ....

(2) ....

(3) ....

Water baptism was not a new rite instituted by John the Baptist. Ceremonial washings were commanded by Moses to prepare the Israelites for the giving of the law on Mt Sinai [Exod 19:10, 14]. When people from neighbouring nations accepted the Jews' religion, they were washed as well as circumcised.

How were the three persons of the Trinity present at Jesus' baptism?

(1) ....

(2) ....

(3) ....

The voice from heaven [11] was one of three such occurrences [also Mark 9:7, John 12:28] when God the Father spoke His approval of the work of His Son.

   John's baptism in the wilderness was a washing which signified true repentance and a putting away of sin. Jesus had nothing of which to repent, but He took His place alongside of sinners in order 'to fulfil all righteousness' [Matt 3:15]. The act of submitting to baptism was also Jesus' dedication to His future ministry.

By Jesus' temptation 1:12, 13 [Parallel passages, Matt 4:1-11, Luke 4:1-13]

Who drove Jesus into the wilderness? ....

How long was He in the wilderness? ....

Who tempted Him? ....

What dangers surrounded Him? ....

Who cared for Him? ....

The Spirit who had descended upon Jesus like a dove at His baptism now drove Him into the wilderness. No sooner had His Father said, 'Thou art my beloved Son,' than Satan challenged Him, 'If thou be the Son of God' [Matt 4:3, 6]. The testing lasted forty days – the same period of time which Moses fasted on Mt Sinai [Exod 34:28] at the second giving of the Ten Commandments, and the length of Elijah's journey to Mt Horeb after the meal which was miraculously supplied to him [I Kings 19:8].

Matthew and Luke describe the temptation in greater detail. First, there was the temptation to satisfy normal bodily hunger; second, the temptation appealing to spiritual pride; and, third, the appeal to personal ambition and power. Into one or other of these three classes all temptations fall. Jesus met the tempter and conquered him by the Word of God, proving that He 'was in all points tempted like as we are, yet without sin' [Heb 4:15].

Beginnings of Jesus' ministry 1:14-45

Introduction 1:14, 15

Time ....

Region .... Ministry ....

Message (*1*) ....

(*2*) ....

(*3*) .... (*4*) ....

Between the events of verses 13 and 14, there is an interval of about fifteen months, concerning which Mark says nothing. He begins his story of Jesus' ministry with the second year, known as 'the year of popularity.' The time is dated by a sad incident, the imprisonment of John the Baptist which marked the end of his public career. Jesus now proclaimed that He was the fulfilment of the prophets' hopes, that the kingdom of God was at hand, and that everyone within the sound of His preaching should repent and believe the gospel. Not only did Jesus preach the gospel; He *was* the gospel.

The first disciples 1:16-20

Place ....

Two sets of brothers...

....

Their occupation................................... Successful? ....

Jesus' call...

Their response ....

Their new occupation ....

These two sets of brothers had been disciples of John the Baptist, but they quickly followed Jesus when convinced He was their Messiah [John 1:35-42]. But it took a special call for them to leave their fishing business on the lake of Galilee to begin 'catching men alive' for Jesus Christ. They obeyed the call immediately and during the rest of Jesus' ministry they never went back to the fishing boats.

Jesus in Capernaum 1:21-34

Day... Place ....

Kind of ministry .... Reaction of people ....

.... Why? ....

....

Deeds of mercy [23-34]

1 In the synagogue [23-28]

Who needed help? ....

How did the demons address Jesus? ....

....

Jesus' rebuke to the demons ....

....

The result ....

The reaction of the people ....

.. ..

Did they gain any understanding of Jesus? ....

If so, what? ....

....

Jesus would not accept the testimony of demons; instead He cast them out. The rebuke, 'Hold thy peace,' means literally, 'Be muzzled,' – a command suitable for a beast.

This first miracle recorded by Mark aroused amazement and astonishment. The reaction of the bystanders was expressed in an exclamation: 'What is this? A new teaching?' More than 'a new teaching,' a new Person whom they should have recognized had come! This Person was the Son of God, their Messiah, and He could exercise authority over evil spirits.

2 In a home [29-31]

Whose home? ....

The emergency ....

....

What did Jesus do? (1) ....

(2) .... (3) ....

The cure ....

This miracle was performed for the sake of His first disciples.

3 On the highway [32-34]

Three classes of people who thronged Peter's door, which probably opened on the

highway (1) ....

(2) .... (3) ....

....

Why did they come? ....

What did Jesus do for them? ....

....

[Compare verse 34b with verses 24, 25]

[6]

Jesus' preparation by.. [35]

When? ....

Where? ....

Jesus interrupted

By whom?.. Why?...

The announcement of Jesus' mission [38] ....

....

'Preaching the gospel of the kingdom of God' [14] was Jesus' most important task at this time; the miracles demonstrated that He was the Son of God.

A leper cleansed [40-45]

Leprosy is perhaps the most loathsome and the most dreaded of diseases. Until recent years there was no known cure. In Old Testament times a leper was banned from his home and community, and left to beg for his living. [Read Lev 13 and 14 for the law concerning lepers.] Each time a leper came near a healthy person, he was required to call out, 'Unclean! Unclean!' just as a warning [Lev 13:44-46].

The leper's faith [40]

Recognition of his need ....

Urgency of his request...

Faith in Jesus' power to heal ....

Question about His willingness to heal...

Jesus' response [41]

Jesus' motive ....

Jesus' method...

Jesus' message...

The cure was instantaneous and complete.

Jesus' directions to the cleansed leper [43, 44]

(*1*) .... (*2*) ....

(*3*) ....

Jesus feared that wide publicity of this miracle would hinder His preaching and teaching. He never wanted His miracles to attract more attention than His words. Therefore, Jesus told the healed man to keep the news to himself. He was sent to the priests to secure official recognition that the cure was real, and to assure the people that Jesus came to fulfil the law.

The leper's disobedience [45] ....

....

Result of disobedience

To Jesus ....

To the multitudes ....

....

REVIEW

Locate each of the following on the map: Judea, Jerusalem, Jordan, Nazareth, Galilee [province], Sea of Galilee, Capernaum.

Look up in a Bible dictionary the following: John the Baptist and the prophet's manner of living; baptism; Sabbath; synagogue; scribes; a leper and his purification.

The key word in this chapter is *authority*.

Authority from whom? .... For what? ....

....

Fill in: Titles of Jesus | By whom given

v I ....

v II ....

v 24 ....

v 24 ....

[8]

Chart the three miracles of healing according to the headings:

Person healed	Place	Need	Jesus' method	Reaction of people

Note what chapter 1 has revealed of the various activities of Jesus' ministry. Find the verse (or verses) which refers to each of the following activities.

Calling of disciples .... Teaching ....

Preaching .... Healing ....

Casting out demons .... Prayer ....

2 Questions and answers

[2:1-3:6]

The miracles of healing brought Jesus widespread popularity. Multitudes thronged Him, coming to Him 'from every quarter.' Amazement and astonishment gripped the people as they tried to explain what was happening before their eyes. And it did not take long for the Jewish religious leaders – scribes and Pharisees – to ask questions which showed their hatred and animosity for the 'new prophet.'

Setting: City .... 'In the house' possibly meant

the home of Peter and Andrew [1:21, 29].

Popularity of Jesus [2, 13] ....

....

Beginnings of opposition

Man sick of the palsy 2:3-12

His condition ....

Difficulty of reaching Jesus ....

His friends – how many? .... What caused them to persist until they

reached Jesus? .... How did they overcome their difficulties?

....

The houses of the East have flat roofs which are reached by an outside staircase. The four friends must have removed some of the loosely laid tiles, and then lowered their friend on his mat-bed by means of ropes. The tiles could easily be replaced later.

Two needs of the sick man (1) ....

(2) ....

With which did Jesus deal first? ....
[10]

How? ....

Reaction of the scribes ....

Jesus' question to the scribes ....

....

Complete restoration ....

Reaction of the general crowd ....

QUESTION I About the forgiveness of sins

Who can forgive sins but God only? asked the scribes.

The scribes were slavish students of the Mosaic law and the teachers of its requirements in the synagogues. They were always assigned the best seats in the synagogue, which added to their importance in the eyes of the people. Their political influence was also great. The scribes of Jesus' day were determined to fit the new Teacher into the pattern of their own interpretations of the law. If He did not conform to their preconceived notions, they simply concluded that He was a bad character and should be put out of the way.

Can you not see, in imagination, a group of scribes 'sitting there' [6] and 'reasoning in their hearts'? Jesus had spoken forgiveness of sins to the palsied man. According to their way of thinking Jesus was pretending to use God's power when He did not really possess it – and that was blasphemy. Furthermore, there was the implication that since there was no outward visible manifestation of the forgiveness of sins, there could be no proof of its reality.

Jesus' answer to these arguments brought another demonstration of His supernatural power. The complete healing [12] of the man should have been proof enough to the scribes that Jesus could both forgive sins and restore health – in other words, Jesus was the Son of God.

The scribes started with the false reasoning that Jesus *could not be* God, and they *were determined not to change* their minds in spite of the evidence.

The call of Matthew [Levi] 2:14, 15

Levi was the son of .... In his own Gospel [Matt 9:9] he refers to himself as 'a man named Matthew.' No doubt, the same man is meant. His original name most likely was Levi. When he was called to be an apostle, he may have received the name Matthew, which means 'gift of God.'

[11]

Matthew belonged to that despised class of men known as ....

One day Jesus found him busily engaged 'at the place of toll.' Here the tax collector levied and collected the taxes on the imports and exports at Capernaum, or the toll on the Roman road which ran through the town.

What was Jesus' call to Matthew? ....

Matthew's response? ....

How did Matthew inform his friends of his new calling and occupation?

....

Who were present? ....

Publicans – the name is derived from Latin – were Jews who became agents of the Roman government to collect taxes for the empire. They had to pay a fixed sum into the treasury, and whatever beyond this they could squeeze out of the people belonged to them. Their unfair dealings caused them to be hated, for they were considered traitors to their own people.

QUESTION II About association with sinners 2:16, 17

The presence of Jesus and His disciples at Matthew's feast caused the scribes and Pharisees to ask another revealing question.

How is it that he [Jesus] eats and drinks with publicans and sinners?

According to Eastern custom, uninvited guests could enter a dining room to observe – or perhaps to pry into – what was going on. Such association of scribes and Pharisees was allowable, whereas eating with them would have been contrary to their interpretation of the Mosaic law. The scribes and Pharisees were implying that when Jesus shared Matthew's hospitality with despised publicans and other notorious sinners, He was no better than they and far below the accepted standards of His critics.

Jesus' answer gave a clear declaration of His purpose in coming into the world [17]. Just as a physician attends the sick to bring help and healing, so Jesus associated with sinners to rescue them from lives of sin. He never overlooked sin, but His purpose was to remove it.

Jesus declared that there were only two classes of people: the *righteous*, and *sinners*. Were the scribes, to whom He was speaking, 'righteous' or were they 'sinners'? That was for them to decide. Those who mistakenly thought they were righteous neither heard nor accepted the call of Christ. How different from Matthew, the publican!

[12]

QUESTION III About fasting 2:19-22

The next question put to Jesus suggests that Matthew's feast may have occurred on a Jewish fast day. The Pharisees boasted of fasting twice a week [Luke 18:12], whereas Moses had commanded only one fast, that on the day of Atonement [Lev 16:29]. John the Baptist by this time was in prison, and his disciples were only expressing their sorrow by their fasting. Both the Pharisees and the disciples of John showed that they were puzzled when they asked Jesus:

Why do the disciples of John and of the Pharisees fast, but thy disciples fast not?

Jesus' answer was given in three parables which contrasted the worn-out ceremonies of the Jewish religion and the new vital spiritual life which He brought. The three illustrations of the wedding feast, the wedding garment, and the wine were suggested naturally by Matthew's feast.

The first parable hints that there is a time to feast and a time to fast. Neither has any merit in itself. To feast is a sign of gladness; to fast is a normal expression of sorrow. It was proper for the disciples of John to fast because they were mourning for their leader who had been thrown into prison. But the presence of Jesus with His disciples called only for rejoicing and feasting because of His daily fellowship with them. He was the Bridegroom, as John had also identified Him, and at whose coming John had rejoiced [John 3:29]. Just as John was taken from his followers the time would come when the Bridegroom [Jesus] would no longer be able to feast with His disciples. When that should happen, fasting would be appropriate.

The suggestion that the Bridegroom 'should be taken away' is a hidden reference [the first in the Gospel of Mark] to Jesus' future death and separation from His disciples.

The second and third parables may be applied to the whole law of Moses in its relation to the gospel. It was just as out of place to try to patch up the old traditions and observances of the scribes and Pharisees by attaching the 'good news' of the gospel to them, as to try to patch up an old coat to make it suitable for a wedding. And it was just as unsuitable to attempt to fit Jesus' message into the old beliefs and practices of Judaism as to fill old dried goat-skin water bottles with new wine, which would be entirely lost as soon as it fermented and burst the brittle wine-skins.

QUESTION IV About the Sabbath 2:23-28

Jesus and His disciples were out walking on the Sabbath, but they were not walking for pleasure. They were on their way to the synagogue [3:1; Matt 12:1-9]. Passing through a corn field on a beaten path, the disciples began to strip off kernels of wheat. They rubbed the kernels in their hands to separate the chaff from the wheat [Luke 6:1], and then ate them to satisfy their hunger.

The Pharisees, still hunting for something to criticize, asked this question:

[13]

Behold, why do they on the sabbath day that which is not lawful?

The disciples were not taking corn that did not belong to them. This was specifically permitted by the law of Moses [Deut 23:25]. On the other hand, the scribes' traditions stated that 'to pluck ears' was *to reap*, and to rub ears in the hand was *to thresh*. These acts were forbidden on the Sabbath.

Jesus' answer was threefold. He appealed, first, to their knowledge of the Old Testament, pointing to an incident in the life of their favourite hero-king, David. [Read I Sam 21:1-6] Fleeing for his life from Saul, David went to the 'house of God' to ask Abiathar, or Ahimelech his father – probably both – for bread for himself and his men. The only bread available was the consecrated bread from the table in God's sanctuary. The law of Moses said that this was to be reserved for priests only, but because of the need of David and his men it was given to them. If David was not blamed for law-breaking, why should not the hungry disciples eat a little raw corn, even if it were contrary to the traditions of the scribes?

With the story of David as a background, Jesus proclaimed a new law of the Sabbath: 'The sabbath was made for man, and not man for the sabbath'. It was designed for the benefit of man – for rest, for worship, for deeds of mercy. It should be man's slave and not his master. Its observances should never deprive him of any necessity; it should not rob him of any benefit. For the disciples to starve on the Sabbath rather than to take the means at their disposal to relieve their hunger would have been a mistaken interpretation of the law of the Sabbath.

Against the authority of the scribes, Jesus asserted the supreme authority of His own Person: 'Therefore the Son of man is Lord also of the sabbath.' He did not abolish the Sabbath, but He reserved the right to interpret it for His disciples.

Man with the withered hand 3:1-6 [This miracle is included with chapter 2 because of its relation to the question of Sabbath-keeping.]

Setting: Place... Day...

The accusers: What did they do? ....

Why? ....

Jesus' first command to the man...

Jesus' questions to the scribes and Pharisees ....

....

....

Jesus' attitudes toward His accusers ....

[14]

Jesus' second command to the man ....

Result ....

Reaction of the Pharisees ....

REVIEW

Look up in a Bible dictionary the following: Pharisees; publicans and taxes, etc; Herodians. [From research on chapter 1, review information concerning Sabbath, scribes, and synagogue.]

Titles of Jesus	By whom given
v 10	....
v 28	....
v 19	....
v 20	....

                    [By parable]

Identify in a sentence, showing how each is related to the events of chapter 2: Levi, Alphaeus, disciples of John, David, Abiathar.

... .

....

....

....

....

From the first two chapters of Mark, note the use of the word *authority*. Find the setting (and reference) for each of the following topics, reviewing the story which proves each point:

Jesus' authority over evil [unclean] spirits ....

....

Jesus' authority over sickness ....

....

Jesus' authority to forgive sin ....

....

Jesus' authority over the Sabbath ....
....

Various reactions to Jesus

Reactions of popularity [2:2, 12, 13, 15] ....
....

Reactions of criticism – 4 Questions

Setting	Question asked	Jesus' answer

I

_____

II

_____

III

_____

IV

_____

Reactions of opposition [3:2, 6] ....
....
....
....
....

[16]

3 *Friends and foes*

[3:7-35]

The public ministry of Jesus opened with a period of tremendous popularity. It was not long, however, before the envy and hatred of the scribes, Pharisees, and Herodians brought about a crisis. Already they were plotting to destroy Him [3:6]. For this reason Jesus quietly slipped out of Capernaum to the shores of the Sea of Galilee.

The multitudes 3:7-12

Setting: Place.................................... People, from where? ....

....

Why had they come? ....

Jesus' wisdom in handling the crowds ....

....

Reasons for the multitudes ....

....

Title given to Jesus ....

By whom?...

This paragraph is characteristic of Mark's writing as he sums up the activity of Jesus' ministry. He vividly pictures the crowds as they 'pressed upon him,' the mighty works, the cry of unclean spirits, and the limitless power of Jesus.

The twelve disciples [apostles] 3:13-19

Jesus' preparation for choosing the twelve [13; see also Luke 6:12] ....

....

Reasons for choosing the twelve (1) ....

[17]

(2) ....

(3) ....

The men

Arrange their names in order of mention, four names in three groups. [Three other lists are given with slightly varying order, Matt 10:2-4; Luke 6:14-16; Acts 1:13.]

.... Name two sets of brothers 1:16-19

....

....

.... What was their previous occupation?

....

.... Matthew (Levi) was the son of

....[2:14],

.... occupation ....

.... and may have been a brother of James,

.... son of Alphaeus.

.... Bartholomew was probably Nathanael

.... of John 1:45.

.... The final name appears last in three

Gospel lists, because he was the

....

Opinions about Jesus 3:19b-22

The excitement of the multitudes mentioned in verses 7 and 8 had not quieted since Jesus' absence. As soon as He returned to Capernaum, the crowds thronged Him again, so much so that He and His disciples could not find time for a hasty meal.

Mistaken friends [family] [21]

Apparently the members of Jesus' family were disturbed by the rumours of His

[18]

great popularity, and a delegation came to see if they could persuade Him to take a rest. Their verdict was '..,' meaning literally, 'He has gone crazy.'

Malicious foes [22]

Scribes who came all the way from Jerusalem to Capernaum made the more serious charge of demon possession. They declared that He was controlled by the pagan god, ..., identified with ....

by the Jews, and that by his power Jesus cast out demons.

Jesus' reply to the scribes 3:23-30

An unanswerable question [23] ....

Further appeal to common sense:

A kingdom divided against itself ....

A household divided ....

Satan divided ....

It is absurd to suggest that Satan is helping Jesus; on the contrary, Jesus is robbing Satan of his power and his property.

A standing offer of forgiveness [28] 'All sins shall be forgiven unto the sons of men, and blasphemies . . .'

The unpardonable sin [29, 30] 'He that shall blaspheme against the Holy Ghost hath never forgiveness, but is in danger of eternal damnation'. The scribes openly charged that Jesus performed His miracles by the power of 'an unclean spirit;' therefore, they spoke in contempt of the Holy Spirit. If they did not repent, there would be no forgiveness for them. Men who wilfully and deliberately blaspheme against the Holy Ghost will never be forgiven. But those who are concerned about the unpardonable sin are the least likely to commit it.

Jesus' true family 3:31-35

Members of Jesus' family were probably as curious about Him as the rest of the multitudes. But they had a deeper reason for wanting to see Him. [See verse 21]

What was it? ....

....

Therefore, His.. and ....

pushed through the crowds, hoping for some personal contact with Him. Up to

this time, it seems that none of His family recognized Him for what He was.

Jesus dismissed the idea of having any special relationship with His mother and

brethren. Instead He offered His own distinct test for relationship in God's family.

Jesus' test [35]: ....

....

....

REVIEW

Locate on map the following: Idumaea, beyond Jordan [Peraea], Tyre, Sidon.

Title of Jesus   By whom given

v 11 ....

Jesus made a careful selection of twelve men from the many who followed Him. Four
of these first appeared in 1:16-20. From this point in Mark's Gospel, look for special
training that Jesus gave them so that they could carry on the work of the gospel after He
was taken from them.

Memorize the names of the Twelve.

Name two sources of opposition to Jesus expressed in this chapter. How did He deal

with it? ....

....

....

Among whom was Jesus most popular? ....

Why? ....

....

[20]

4 Parables

[4:1-34]

A parable is the illustration of truth by the use of a picture taken from common experience. It has also been described as an 'earthly story with a heavenly meaning.' This kind of teaching was popular with the Jewish rabbis. Jesus used the method so that His friends and disciples would understand better the significance of His kingdom and His message. His enemies, on the other hand, could not grasp the meaning of what He was trying to tell them.

The following poem shows very simply how Jesus used parables in teaching.

> He talked of grass, and wind and rain,
> Of fig trees and fair weather;
> And made it His delight to bring
> Heaven and earth together.
>
> He spoke of lilies, vines and corn,
> The sparrow and the raven;
> And words so natural, yet so wise,
> Were on men's hearts engraven.
>
> Of yeast with bread, and flax and cloth,
> Of eggs, and fish and candles;
> See how the whole familiar world
> He most divinely handles!

Two other definitions of a parable may be illustrated from Mark's Gospel.

(1) It has been called 'a short pithy saying.' See Mark 7:14-17.

(2) It is sometimes a comparison without a narrative, as, for example, 'Now learn a parable of the fig tree . . .' [Mark 13:28].

In comparison with the other three Gospels, Mark contains many miracles, but few parables. Nevertheless, those that do appear are important, and one of them in this chapter [the parable of the growing seed] is found only in Mark.

Setting [4:1, 2]: Number of people ....

Jesus' pulpit .... Teaching by ....

The parable of the soils (sower) 4:3–9, 14–20

'Hearken ... He that hath ears to hear, let him hear' [4:3, 9]. Since Jesus was beginning a new method of teaching, He called attention to it at the beginning and at the end of the first parable.

Copy neatly the parable and its interpretation in the two parallel columns below. [Suggestions for omitting less essential phrases are indicated]

The parable	The interpretation
(3) There went	(14) The sower ....
....	
(4) Some fell	(15) But when they have heard, ...
....	....
....	....
....	....
(5) And some fell	(16) When they have heard....................
....	....
....	....
....	....
(6)	(17) And have no root...........................
....	....
....	....
....	....
....	....
(7) And some fell	(18) Such as hear the word,...................
....	(19) And the cares of this world ....
....	....

(8) And other fell on.......... .... (20) Such as hear the word,................

This parable was spoken to the .... [1] but

its interpretation was revealed to a smaller group of ....

.... [10]. In all the cases mentioned there were the

same sower and the same seed. Only the various conditions of the soil account for

the different results.

The purpose of the parable 4:10-13

To the Twelve and other followers of Jesus, the parable was spoken that they
might 'know the mystery of the kingdom of God' [11]. To those 'on the outside'
the parable was given so that they would not understand. Listening to Jesus'
teaching, there were always two classes of people. Some heard and understood;
others heard and were completely mystified.

A 'mystery' means not something which is impossible to understand, but a
truth formerly hidden and now revealed. 'The mystery of the kingdom' was
something into which the disciples were initiated by Jesus, therefore known to
them and hidden from others.

The responsibility of those who receive the Word 4:21-25

Jesus was unwilling that the parable of the soils and the further 'mysteries of the
kingdom' which He would reveal should be kept secret. He intended that the
disciples would proclaim them openly to the world. To illustrate this truth,
Jesus used two short parables based upon every-day living.

Each Galilean home had its lamp [candle], its bed, and its corn measure [bushel].
Anyone could see the folly of first lighting the lamp and then hiding it under the

corn measure or the couch-bed. It should be placed on a lampstand, where it will shed the greatest light.

Just so, Jesus expected His followers who received the Word of the gospel to become beacons to illuminate the world.

Then Jesus changed His illustration, perhaps thinking of the corn measure in each home. As the disciples had received the Word, so they were to give it out, just as they would measure out corn to the hungry from their own abundant corn supply.

The Word of the gospel, then, is both light for the world's darkness and food for the hungry multitudes. Its supply is never exhausted; the only danger of loss comes from not giving it away!

The parable of the growing seed 4:26-29

This parable is found only in Mark's Gospel. It might be given the title, 'The parable of secret growth,' for that is the purpose of its teaching.

Fill in the equivalent statements from the story to explain the following outline.

The seed is sown ....

The growth is unaided by man ....

....

The growth is gradual ....

The harvest is apparent ....

The reaping completes the life purpose of the seed..

....

The parable of the mustard seed 4:30-34

The size of the mustard seed ....

A full-grown mustard tree ....

....

'Small as a grain of mustard seed,' was a Jewish proverb. 'A stalk of mustard seed,' wrote one rabbi, 'was in my garden, into which I used to climb, as men do into a fig-tree.' The same principle of growth from the tiniest of seeds to a mustard tree 'as tall as the horse and its rider' [W. M. Thomson] represents the spread of the Word of the gospel. From the smallest beginning nineteen hundred years ago, it now reaches around the globe. This parable also represents the noticeable change from a young believer into a grown-up mature Christian.

REVIEW

What is a parable? What is its purpose as a form of teaching?

Explain 4:33, 34.

The parable of the soils points out the responsibility of those who hear the Word.

The parable of the growing seed shows the right attitude for those who proclaim the Word.

The parable of the mustard seed pictures the outward growth resulting from the proclamation and hearty reception of the Word.

It takes all three parables to explain the 'mystery of the kingdom.'

Explain briefly the four kinds of soil and the different types of hearers they represent.

I ....   I ....

....

2 ....   2 ....

....

3 ....   3 ....

....

4 ....   4 ....

What is the chief idea expressed by the parable of the growing seed?

5 Miracles

[4:35-41; 5:1-43]

Following a long day of teaching by parables, Jesus sought refuge on 'the other side' of the lake.

Stilling the storm 4:35-41

Preparation for the trip [36] ....

....

The sudden storm ....

The immediate danger ....

Jesus' apparent unconcern ....

The disciples' despair ....

....

Jesus' command to the storm ....

Jesus' rebuke to the disciples ....

....

The disciples' reaction to Jesus ....

....

....

This miracle showed Jesus' authority over nature.

Once again Jesus and His disciples crossed the Sea of Galilee. On this occasion they landed in a thinly populated spot where a steep cliff rose high above the water. The hillsides were full of caves for tombs which to this day are used for burial places. Wild hogs still pasture in this barren land. As the Master's boat touched shore, Jesus was approached by one who desperately needed His help.

Healing of the demoniac 5:1-20

The demoniac 1-10

His home ....

His physical condition ....

....

His actions ....

....

His approach to Jesus ....

His address to Jesus ....

....

....

Name given to the spirits ....

The deliverance 11-14 ....

From a bad name [reputation] ....

From a host of demons ....

The results 15-17

For the man ....

For the demons ....

For the swine...

For the swine-keepers ....

For Jesus...

Jesus' interview with the delivered demoniac 18-20

The man's request..

Request refused ....

Jesus' command...

....

Result of his testimony.. ......

....

Jesus now directed His little ship back to the west side of the lake, where new multitudes awaited His help.

An urgent request 5:21-24

A ruler of the synagogue

His name ....

His attitude toward Jesus...

His great trouble ....

His request of Jesus ....

....

His faith ....

Jesus' response ....

Immediate ....

Interrupted [25-34] ....

....

The sick woman 5:25-34

The woman

Length of illness ....

Failure of physicians..

Money spent in vain...

Hopelessness of case ....

The woman's contact with Jesus

Faith [28] ....

Action [27]..
[28]

Three steps in her faith

Imperfect, because of trust in the magic of touching Jesus [28]

Challenged to acknowledge what she had done [33]

Complete, with Jesus' words of healing and peace [34]

The raising of Jairus' daughter 5:35-43

The ruler's faith tested

By delay [25-34] ....

By death ....

By mourning ....

The ruler's faith rewarded 36-41

Jesus' words of assurance

(1) .... [36]

(2) .... [39]

Jesus' trusted helpers ....

Jesus' command to the daughter ....

Effect of the miracle 42

Upon the daughter ....

Upon the friends and mourners ....

Jesus' command 43

On behalf of the daughter ....

On behalf of Himself ....

REVIEW

Tell the story of the stilling of the storm centred around these three questions:

'Carest thou not that we perish?'

'How is it that ye have no faith?' [Revised Version, 'Have ye not yet faith?']

'What manner of man is this, that even the wind and the sea obey him?'

By whom were these questions asked, and to whom were they addressed?

What does this incident tell you about the disciples?

What new thing did you learn about Jesus?

Titles of Jesus	By whom given
4:38	....
5:7	....
5:35	....

Locate on map: Decapolis [meaning Ten Cities]; country of the Gadarenes [chief city, Gadara].

Identify: Peter, James, and John (as a unit).

Look up in a Bible dictionary: ruler of a synagogue.

Make a chart of the four miracles according to the following suggestions: (the completed first line will show you how to answer the rest)

	Storm	Legion	Woman	Ruler's daughter
Jesus' power over	Nature	Demons	Disease	Death
Need for help				
Attitude to Jesus before miracle				
after miracle				
Expression of faith				
Extent of recovery				
Results to Jesus' ministry				

[30]

What do these miracles reveal about Christ?

What four classes of people were affected?

In this section Jesus is called 'the Master' [Teacher]. Search for other occurrences of the word in chapters 5, 9, 10, 11, 12, 13, 14.

6 Opinions – pro and con

[6:1-56]

Jesus now left the vicinity of Capernaum and 'came into his own country,' [the Greek word used means 'fatherland'] the district of Nazareth where He had been brought up. There lived His mother, Mary, with other sons and daughters. What kind of a welcome did He receive?

Rejection in Nazareth 6:1-6

Setting: Place.................................... Day ....:..

What was Jesus doing in the synagogue? ....

Various reactions

Astonishment..

Recognized His wisdom ....

Recalled His miracles ....

Rejected His claims ....

Reasons for rejection

Familiarity. The townspeople knew Him and His family.

False standards of greatness. The people said with a sneer, 'He's only a carpenter.'

Unknown as to His real identity. Even a prophet escapes notice in His own home town.

Unbelief. This is the underlying reason for all other wrong conclusions about Christ.

Because of the hostility of Nazareth, Jesus' ministry was greatly hindered.

A few sick folk were ...., but He could perform no ....

.... Nevertheless, He faithfully continued His ....

.... in the nearby villages.

Mission of the twelve 6:7-13

It was impossible for Jesus to go to all the towns and cities in Palestine during His brief earthly ministry, so He trained the twelve disciples to assist Him. He had already selected them [3:14, 15]. Since that time they had been 'with him,' [observing all that He said and did] – now they were to be *apostles* or 'sent ones.'

Special instructions to the twelve

Strategy [order of going]..

Commission [see also Matt 10:7, 8] (1) ....

.... [12] (2) ....

(3) .... [13]

Equipment

What not to take ....

....

What to take...

These instructions implied that the disciples were to go on their journey without special preparations, but as the ordinary Galilean peasant would travel.

Hospitality

Welcome [10] ....

Unwelcome [11] ....

....

Progress of the mission [12, 13] (1) ....

(2) .... (3) ....

(4) ....

Report to Jesus [30] (1) ....

(2) ....

Jesus knew that there would be the same two reactions to the disciples' preaching tour that He always experienced. Some would hear them gladly; others would refuse to hear in spite of the witness of miracles added to their message. To those who refused, the apostles were instructed to use the common Jewish sign of renunciation – that of shaking off the dust under their feet, an example which Paul and Barnabas followed later at Antioch [Acts 13:51, see also 18:6; compare Nehemiah 5:13].

[33]

More opinions about Jesus 6:14-16

Herod's opinion..

Other opinions (1).. (2) ....

(3) ....

Why was Herod so sure that Jesus was John the Baptist returned? ....

....

[This particular Herod, known as Antipas, was a grandson of Herod the Great who slew the young children of Bethlehem [Matt chap. 2]. Philip, also mentioned in the story, was his half-brother.]

The death of John the Baptist 6:17-29

Retell in your own words the story of the events leading to the death of John the Baptist. Keep in mind these two questions: Did Herod have a conscience? Which person [or persons] in the story was chiefly responsible for the death of John?

....

....

....

....

....

....

....

....

....

....

[6: 17–29]
....

Jesus' invitation to his disciples 6:30-34

Disciples' report of their mission [30] ....

....

[34]

Jesus' invitation to the disciples [31] ....

....

Why? ....

Where did they go? ....

Their rest interrupted ....

What Jesus saw ....

What Jesus felt ....

Why? ....

Feeding the five thousand 6:35-44

Time of day ....

The embarrassing situation ....

Disciples' solution ....

Jesus' command ....

Disciples' inadequate supplies ....

....

The miracle 39-44

Organization ....

Giving thanks ....

Distribution ....

Satisfaction ....

Over-supply ....

Number fed ....

This miracle marks the peak of Jesus' popularity. It is reported by all four Gospel writers [Matt 14:14-21; Luke 9:12-17; John 6:5-13], showing its importance and significance in Jesus' ministry. John chapter 6 gives us a sermon based on the miracle.

Jesus walking on the water 6:45-52

Disciples dismissed ....

People sent away ....

Jesus alone – where? .... Why? ....

Disciples alone

Place .... Their trouble ....

....

Jesus' knowledge of their trouble ....

Jesus' help ....

Reaction of the disciples (1) ....

(2) ....

Why? ....

According to the Roman division of 'watches' Jesus approached the tossing boat between 3 and 6 o'clock in the morning. Presumably the disciples had been rowing against heavy winds and high waves for about nine hours and had progressed only halfway across the lake – a distance of three miles or less. The situation looked hopeless until Jesus appeared.

When Jesus proved for the second time His power over nature, the hearts of the disciples were still so sluggish [not stony] that they could not fully comprehend who He was. It was not long since He had fed 5,000 people and they ought to have realized that, if He could miraculously feed the hungry, He was able to meet any emergency.

Ministry in Gennesaret 6:53-56

[A small but very fertile plain to the north-west of the Sea of Galilee]

Jesus' widespread popularity ....

What was the people's chief interest in Jesus? ....

....

How did Jesus meet their needs? ....

....

....

[36]

The desire of the sick to touch the hem of Jesus' garment reminds one of what miracle? [See Mark 5] ....

REVIEW

Locate on map: Jesus' 'own country', Bethsaida; the 'sea'; Gennesaret.

Opinions about the identity of Jesus

By fellow-townsmen [3]	Why? [6]
By Herod [14]	Why?
By 'others' [15]	Why?

Various reactions to Jesus

By people of Nazareth	Why?
By disciples [51]	Why?
By people of Gennesaret [54]	Why?

Note Jesus' need for privacy and prayer, and His recognition of the same for the disciples [31, 46]. Christians today need to take time for thinking about God and His Son, and for using their privilege of prayer. See Matthew 6:6.

7 Opposition – traditions
[7:1-37]

As Jesus' popularity reached its height, there was growing opposition by the scribes and Pharisees who came from Jerusalem with the intention of trapping Him. At this time the religious leaders of the Jews posed another in a series of questions to determine whether or not the teaching and practice of Jesus were in accordance with their own principles. [See chapter 2 for four questions previously raised.]

QUESTION V About the tradition of eating with unwashed hands 7:1-23

The Jews demanded two kinds of washings: [1] for the sake of cleanliness; and [2] to remove ceremonial impurity. The ceremonial washing was not required by the law of Moses, but was added later as 'the tradition of the elders' which became more binding than the original law.

Thus, when a Jew returned from market, it was considered a religious duty to wash his hands before eating. It was also a duty to clean by a religious ceremony all cups and pots, cooking vessels and furniture, before using them.

The scribes and Pharisees no doubt waited for an occasion to observe the practice of the disciples, and when they caught them eating with ceremonially unwashed hands, 'they found fault.' Then they asked Jesus this pointed question:

> Why walk not thy disciples according to the tradition of the
> elders, but eat bread with unwashen hands?

Jesus' answer. Jesus was not slow to call these scribes and Pharisees 'hypocrites' and emphasized the fact by quoting from one of the Old Testament prophets who described them accurately.

> This people honoureth me with their lips,
> But their heart is far from me;
> Howbeit in vain do they worship me,
> Teaching for doctrines the commandments of men.
> [Mark 7:6, 7, quoting Isaiah 29:13]

A hypocrite originally meant one who acted a part on a stage, and who perhaps wore a mask to hide his identity. It denotes one who assumes a character which does not really belong to him, or acts a part that is unreal. The persons to whom Jesus applied the word *hypocrite* approached God with their lips while their hearts were far from Him. They were acting the part of true worshippers, but were not

[38]

so in reality. They wore a mask of profession which they put on to hide their real character.

The second sin of the scribes and Pharisees was to take the traditions of men more seriously than the commandments of God. Jesus illustrated what He meant by calling their attention to the Fifth Commandment – 'Honour thy father and thy mother' [Exod 20:12] – and the further warning of Moses, 'He that curseth his father, or his mother, shall surely be put to death' [Exod 21:17]. If a Jewish son wished to avoid the obligation to provide for his parents, he had only to pronounce the word *Corban* over his possessions to free himself from any responsibility [7:11].

'Corban' meant anything dedicated to God. The traditions provided that any property thus given to God could not be given to any other person, but it could be used by its owner for his own personal gratification.

Anyone would have to admit that this practice was entirely inconsistent with any true profession of godliness. 'And,' charged Jesus, 'many such like things do ye' [7:13].

The difference between outward and inward uncleanness 14-23

Jesus now widened the circle of listeners, for His teaching was not only for the Pharisees, though their question prompted the discussion. Link verses 15 and 21, 22:

There is nothing from without a man, that entering into him can defile him; but the things which come out of him, those are they that defile the man. . . . For from within, out of the heart of men, proceed evil thoughts, adulteries, fornications, murders, thefts, covetousness, wickedness, deceit, lasciviousness (lust), an evil eye (envy), blasphemy, pride, foolishness.

In other words, no one is made unclean by what goes into his mouth, but by that which comes from his heart. Why be so petty and particular to wash cups and cooking pots and hands? No one is polluted by eating something considered ceremonially unclean, but only by thinking and doing that which is morally unclean.

Verse 24 marks a transition. Jesus now visited outside Galilee as He entered the territory belonging to Tyre and Sidon. [Some think, however, that Mark's words mean the remote part of Galilee bordering on the territory of Tyre and Sidon.] The religious leaders of the Jews seemed to be united in a campaign of hate against Him, which caused Him to seek semi-retirement from the curious crowds. Mark explains the situation in a few short words, 'he could not be hid,' even though He longed for rest and for greater opportunity to prepare His disciples for what lay ahead of them all.

[39]

The Syrophoenician woman 7:24-30

The woman

Her nationality ....

Her trouble ....

Her attitude toward Jesus..

Her faith..

Jesus' test of the woman's faith

What did Jesus mean in verse 27? [Remember that this woman was a Gentile. Take the word 'children' to mean 'the Jews,' and 'dogs' to stand for 'Gentiles.' The word used by Jesus signifies 'little dogs'; it means, not the rough wild dogs that prowled the streets, but the small dogs attached to households.] ....

....

....

The woman's answer

What did she mean?..

....

Jesus' reply

Faith honoured ....

Effect upon daughter ....

This miracle shows clearly that although Jesus came in the first place to the Jewish nation in fulfilment of God's promise, His message and His works were for Gentiles, too.

The deaf and dumb man 7:31-37

Jesus now left.. and came to ....

travelling through the area known as .... [10 cities]

The man's need..

His friends' request ....

Jesus' method of healing ....

....

[40]

Results to the man ....

....

Results in the community ....

....

....

REVIEW

Locate on map: Tyre, Sidon.

Identify: Esaias [Isaiah].

Look up in Bible dictionary: Corban.

Title of Jesus   By whom given

v 28 ....

QUESTION V asked Jesus by the Pharisees; Jesus' answers.

Fill in the chart concerning the two miracles in this chapter.

	Daughter	Deaf man
Nationality		
Need		
Faith of whom?		
Jesus' method		
Result		

8 Peter's confession

[8:1-38]

The wide publicity given to the healing of the deaf man [7:36] again brought the multitudes to listen to the Master's teaching. They were so anxious to hear that they forgot to provide for themselves necessary food. Whatever small supplies they might have brought were exhausted three days later. Jesus' concern for the people moved Him to perform another outstanding miracle, second only to the feeding of the five thousand reported in Mark 6:34-44.

The feeding of the four thousand 8:1-10

By means of the following chart, compare the two miracles of feeding the multitudes.

	5,000 [6:34-44]	4,000 [8:1-9]
Jesus' concern [compassion] for the multitudes		
Time spent with Jesus		
Place		
Supplies on hand		
Jesus' method		
Left-overs		

An impertinent question 8:10-13

After the miracle of feeding four thousand people, Jesus crossed the lake again to the western shore of the Sea of Galilee. The Pharisees quickly found out His presence and eagerly sought to renew their attack upon Him.

For what did the Pharisees ask? ....

What greater sign could Jesus have given them than the feeding of the multitudes, the healing of the sick, and the casting out of demons? The Pharisees apparently wanted a 'sign from heaven' such as Elijah's fire from heaven which burned up his sacrifice [1 Kings 18:21-39]. But Jesus knew that even if He complied with their request, the Pharisees would not be convinced. Note particularly the description of Jesus' sorrow caused by their unbelief. ....

Jesus' refusal of the Pharisees' request ....

....

Jesus abruptly left the Pharisees and sailed with His disciples to the other side of the lake.

The leaven of the Pharisees and of Herod 8:14-21

Situation: .... [14]

Jesus' warning to the disciples..

....

Disciples' misunderstanding..

Reasons for misunderstanding..

....

[The disciples' minds were occupied by thoughts of material bread while Jesus was talking about spiritual truths. If they needed food, one loaf of bread would have been more than enough in view of the two miracles of feeding vast multitudes. Could the disciples forget so easily? Could they fail to understand?]

Jesus, no doubt, referred to the hypocrisy of the Pharisees and the worldliness of the Herodians [see Matt 16:12] and to the insistence upon unnecessary traditions. But the disciples did not yet comprehend the full meaning of this bit of teaching by parable.

The blind man of Bethsaida 8:22-26

This miracle is recorded only by Mark, and is unusual because of the two-stage cure of the man.

How did the man get to Jesus? ....

The request ....

Jesus' method of treatment ....

....

Evidence of partial healing ....

Treatment continued ....

Result ....

Jesus' word of caution ....

....

Peter's great confession 8:27-33

Setting: Place..

Jesus' great question ....

Varied answers (1)..

(2) .... (3) ....

Peter's great confession ....

Jesus' word of caution to disciples ....

Jesus' great announcement (1) ....

(2) .... (3) ....

(4) ....

Reaction of Peter ....

Jesus' great rebuke of Peter ....

....

There have been earlier hints in this Gospel of Jesus' death. But the time was getting much nearer when all these things *must* take place, and Jesus began to prepare His disciples for the coming trial.

[44]

Tests of discipleship 8:34-38 [Memorize these five verses]

Give the threefold test of discipleship [34]

(1) ....

(2) ....

(3) ....

The Christian who denies himself does not give up some one or other thing for Christ; he gives up himself – all his ambitions and desires – to put Christ first in his heart and life. See Proverbs 23:26 and Matthew 6:33.

The Christian must also take up his cross of suffering and shame as he witnesses for his Lord.

Finally, the Christian is to follow his Lord, to death if need be – for that is where Jesus was going when He spoke these words.

Just as a business man calculates his income by assets and liabilities, so life may be counted as profit or loss. See what Jesus had to say about it.

Worldly profit	*Heavenly loss*
Save life here	Lose life hereafter
Gain world here	Lose soul hereafter
Ashamed of Jesus here	Jesus ashamed of us hereafter

'But whosoever shall lose his life for my sake and the gospel's, the same shall save it.'

REVIEW

Locate on map: Caesarea Philippi; Bethsaida.

Three instances of lack of understanding of Jesus' purpose and ministry.

Pharisees [11] ....

....

Disciples [17-21] ....

....

....

[45]

Peter [32, 33] ....

....

....

Title of Jesus   **By whom given**

v 29 ....

[46]

9 Transfiguration

[9:1-50]

The first verse of Mark 9 links Mark 8:38 with 9:2. Jesus spoke of Himself as coming 'in the glory of his Father' and 'with power.' This promise Peter connected with the transfiguration for he wrote many years later in his epistle [2 Pet 1:16-18]:

> For we have not followed cunningly devised fables, when we made known unto you the *power* and *coming* of our Lord Jesus Christ, but were eyewitnesses of his majesty. For he received from God the Father honour and glory, when there came such a voice to him from the excellent glory, This is my beloved Son, in whom I am well pleased. And this voice which came from heaven we heard, when we were with him in the holy mount.

The transfiguration 9:2-8

Setting: Time .... [the discourse recorded in 8:34-38]

Place .... [probably the lower slopes of Hermon, a mountain 9,100 feet high, and visible from every part of Palestine.]

Those present..

The vision of glory – 'He was transfigured before them.'

Description of glory...

....

The transfiguration [metamorphosis] was a *transformation* as startling as the difference between an unused electric light bulb and one in which the light shines through. The glory of God belonged to Jesus during His earthly life, but it was concealed by His human body. On the Mount of Transfiguration, Jesus allowed that glory to shine through His body, so that His disciples would never again doubt that He was the Son of God. His moral glory, ever present, was seen by the eye of faith alone.

Two visitors ....

These two heavenly visitors represented the law and the prophets.

Peter's proposal..

....

Effect of vision on disciples ....

....

The Father's blessing ....

....

The vision of Jesus ....

....

Moses and Elijah disappeared as quickly as they had come, leaving only Jesus visible to the three disciples. The Son had come to fulfil the law and the prophets, and the disciples must now pay attention to His every word as He began to speak more openly about His death and resurrection.

Descent from the mountain 9:9-13

Jesus' charge to the disciples ....

....

Disciples' obedience ....

Disciples' questionings

(1) .... [10]

(2) .... [11]

Jesus' reply

The Son of man *must suffer* many things.

Elijah had already come in the person of John the Baptist, fulfilling the prophecy of Malachi 4:5. Just as John suffered death at the hands of Herod and Herodias [6:17-29], so Jesus would undergo scorn, rejection, and physical suffering at His trial and crucifixion. This was most difficult for the disciples to comprehend.

The demoniac boy 9:14-29

Jesus and three disciples rejoin...

[48]

Four groups represented (1) ....

(2) .... (3) ....

(4) ....

Questionings: By whom? ....

Why? ....

Need of the boy

Actions of the boy ....

....

Length of time of his affliction ....

Disciples' failure ....

The father's faith

Bringing son to Jesus ....

Faith tested by disciples' failure ....

Germ of faith in Jesus' ability ....

Jesus' response 23-27 ....

Jesus' challenge to the father's faith ....

....

The father's confession and prayer..

....

Rebuke of the demons...

Deliverance from demons ....

Complete healing ....

Disciples' dilemma 28, 29

Question asked of Jesus ....

[49]

[When Jesus sent the disciples on their missionary tour, He gave them 'power over unclean spirits' and they reported that they had 'cast out many devils,' (demons) Mark 6:7, 13.]

Jesus' answer ....

....

[Jesus never made prayer and fasting a requirement as an exercise or ritual, but rather a challenge to faithfulness of intercession and self-discipline.]

Going through Galilee 9:30-32

Jesus' desire for seclusion ....

Jesus' second prediction concerning Himself (1) ....

.... (2) ....

(3) ....

Reactions of disciples (1) ....

(2) ....

The disciples still dreamed of an earthly kingdom which Messiah would establish. Repeated teaching was necessary to make them ready for the suffering and death which would soon overtake their Master. Not until after the resurrection and the coming of the Holy Spirit at Pentecost, did they fully understand.

Jesus, teaching His disciples 9:33-50

Setting: Place............................... Dispute among disciples ....

....

Jesus' answer [35] ....

....

Don't try to be 'first' – be humble.

Jesus meant that if anyone wants to be first, he must be willing to be the last of all and the servant of all. Compare with the words given in Mark the more detailed instruction given in Matthew 18:1-5 and the similar teaching given in Luke 9:46-48. Selfless humility is pleasing to the Lord; the desire 'to be someone' issues from pride. True greatness is being willing to take a humble place in order to serve others.

[50]

This discussion reminded John of a recent happening. What had the disciples observed? [38] ....

....

How did they feel about this? ....

....

Jesus' answer [39, 40] ....

....

....

The disciple must ever remember the Lord's words: Judge not that ye be not judged' [see Matthew 7:1-3].

There is no place for jealousy or prejudice among the followers of Christ. All service which is done sincerely in the name of Christ is acceptable and pleasing to the Lord. This service need not be great, like the casting out of demons, to prove one's loyalty. Just a cup of water – to use Jesus' illustration – given in the name of Christ to one who belongs to Him will be rewarded.

Jesus now turned the conversation back to consider the little child who was in His arms. For, whoever will cause one of these little ones – or any young believer –

to stumble, 'it is better for him ....

....

....

Don't be stumbling blocks – be examples.

The hand, foot, and eye are symbols of *doing, going,* and *seeing* and *thinking.* If certain habits of life cause us, or those with whom we come in contact, to turn away from God, they must be cast away. It is necessary either to discipline our-selves or to face everlasting judgment. Jesus used strong language when He talked about hell and hell fire, alluding to Isaiah 66:24. There the prophet described the fate of those who transgress against God, for they are cast out where worms and continually burning fires destroy their bodies.

How much better to be 'an example of the believers, in word, in conversation, in charity [love], in spirit, in faith, in purity' as Paul counselled Timothy [1 Tim 4:12]!

Both fire and salt preserve and purify. They preserve from corruption and purify for future usefulness. Both figures of speech represent self-discipline, which is often painful and severe. Salt which has lost its saltiness is useless. Therefore, Jesus cautioned His followers, 'Be sure to be genuine salt.' One who disciplines himself will never have to be disciplined by another.

See how skilfully Jesus took the thoughts of the disciples back to the dispute about who would be the greatest. If they practised humility, love, forbearance, and self-discipline, they would not be contending about which of them would have the place of prominence in the kingdom. Instead they would enjoy peace and harmony with one another.

REVIEW

Locate on map: Mt Hermon, Capernaum, Galilee [province].

Compare the records of the transfiguration of Jesus: Mark 9:1-8, Matthew 17:1-9, and Luke 9:28-36. Note especially the description of 'glory' in each.

What predictions did Jesus make concerning Himself that were fulfilled in His lifetime? List them.

What teachings did Jesus give His disciples at this time? What prompted the discussion?

Titles of Jesus	By whom given
v 5	....
v 7	....
v 9	....
v 12	....
v 17	....
v 24	....
v 31	....
v 38	....
v 41	....

10 *Interviews*

[10:1-52]

This chapter marks the turning-point in Jesus' ministry. He closed the public preaching, healing, and teaching tours in Galilee where He had always enjoyed a degree of popularity. He set His face toward the suffering and death which He knew were inevitable, and travelled towards Jerusalem where the hatred of the Jews would manifest itself to the fullest extent.

On His way to Jerusalem, Jesus was still as concerned as ever for those in physical or spiritual need and He was always prepared to help them. He never let His own sufferings interfere with His service to others.

Interview with the Pharisees 10:1-12

The Pharisees were ever looking for a way to discredit Jesus as a teacher. On this occasion they raised a question about a subject which was of the highest importance to the Jews. The rabbis were divided in their opinions concerning marriage and divorce. Some of them held that a man might divorce his wife for almost any whim or prejudice. Others maintained the sacredness of marriage and would allow divorce only for unfaithfulness. Both of these views were probably represented by the Pharisees as they asked another question – the sixth in a series [see chapters 2 and 7].

QUESTION VI About divorce

Is it lawful for a man to put away his wife?

Jesus' question in answer to the Pharisees' question..

....

The Pharisees' answer ....

Jesus' explanation of Moses' law

Sin had spoiled the original intention ....

....

God's original intention for marriage

God made both man and woman ....

Man and woman were made for each other...

....

The two were to become one..

The union to endure as long as life lasted...

The puzzled disciples ....

Jesus' pronouncement on divorce ....

....

....

Compare this passage with Matthew 5:32, 19:9. In God's sight, the tie of marriage may be broken only by death or by the sin of unfaithfulness. To remarry under any other condition is to commit the great sin of adultery.

Jesus and little children 10:13-16

It was customary among the Jews for mothers to ask famous teachers to lay their hands in blessing upon the heads of their children. Those who brought their children to Jesus, then, were acting according to their custom.

The disciples' attitude toward children ....

....

Jesus' attitude toward His disciples...

....

Jesus' attitude toward children ....

....

Children as an object lesson..

....

What Jesus did for the children (1) ....

(2) .... (3) ....

[Re-read 9:36-37]

Interview with the rich young ruler 10:17-22

The young man's attitude to Jesus

His acts ....

His salutation ....

His question ....

Jesus' answer [in two parts]

(1) ....

(2) ....

....

....

Young man's reply ....

Jesus' dealing with the young man's need

His feeling toward him ....

His diagnosis of his need ....

His prescription for the remedy ....

....

....

[Underline the verbs in the imperative]

The young man's reaction

His feelings..

His actions ....

The reason for both his feelings and actions...

....

....

Jesus' comment on riches 10:23-27

Did Jesus mean that no rich man would enter the kingdom of God? ....

A common Jewish proverb [25] ....

....

....

What did Jesus mean? Could 'trust in riches' [24] be the clue?...............................

....

....

Jesus' definition of 'following' Him 10:28-31

Peter was thinking of Jesus' command to the rich young ruler, 'Follow me' [10:21], when he declared, 'Lo, we have left all, and have followed thee.' Perhaps he had in mind his fishing business which was his source of income, or members of his family. 'Shall we be any better off than the rich young ruler?' mused Peter, the spokesman for the rest of the disciples.

Here is Jesus' definition of 'following':

If you leave ....

....

for my sake and the gospel's sake, you will receive now ....

....

....

with ...., and in the world to come you will receive

....

Don't forget the warning: 'Many that are first now shall be last then, and last now will be first then.'

Jesus' prediction concerning Himself 10:32-34

Setting: Where? ....

Feelings of the disciples ....

[56]

Twice before [8:31, 9:31] Jesus had spoken definitely of his future sufferings.

What information did Jesus repeat? ....

....

....

What additional details did He give in 10:33, 34? ....

....

....

....

Interview with James and John 10:35-45

Who were James and John? ....

They came to Jesus with a special personal request.

The request of ambition ....

....

The rebuke of ambition

Honours must be received through suffering [38] ....

....

....

Honours are awarded to the worthy according to the good pleasure of God [40]

....

....

The 'cup' and the 'baptism' of which Jesus spoke [38] both referred to the ordeal of pain and suffering which He was facing.

The remedy for ambition

The need for a remedy – personal jealousy among the disciples [41] ....

....

....

The wrong path to power for disciples – the assertion of power and authority over others, illustrated by Gentile rulers [42]..

....

The true path of honour

Service [43, 44] ....

Jesus, our example [45] ....

....

....

Memorize Mark 10:45, for it is the key to the life of Christ portrayed in this Gospel: 'Even the Son of Man came not to be ministered unto, but to minister [serve], and to give his life a ransom for many'.

Interview with blind Bartimaeus 10:46–52

Setting: Place.. on the way to ....

People present ....

The man

His name .... His father ....

His plight .... His occupation ....

The man's faith

His faith in whom? ....

His faith expressed ....

His faith challenged ....

His faith re-expressed ....

The man's faith honoured

Jesus' response ....

The bystanders' help...

The man's action ....

[58]

Jesus' question ....

The man's answer ....

Sight restored...

Result: a 'follower' ....

REVIEW

Locate on map: Judaea, Jordan [river], Jerusalem, Jericho, Nazareth.

In chapter 10 Jesus has been dealing with individuals or small groups. Can you account for this change?

Titles of Jesus	By whom given
v 17	....
v 20	....
v 33	....
v 35	....
v 45	....
v 47	....
v 47, 48	....
v 51	....

Compare and contrast Jesus' interviews with the rich young ruler and with Bartimaeus.

	Ruler	Bartimaeus
Question asked of Jesus		
Jesus' reply	[command]	[action]
Man's response		
Result		

11 *Authority*

[11:1-12:12]

Chapter 11 marks the beginning of the last week of the earthly life of Jesus. From this point on, each event and each bit of teaching has a greater significance as the story rushes headlong toward the crucifixion. Mark, the author, recognized this and devoted approximately one third of his Gospel to the final week of Jesus' life. The start of the last sad journey to Jerusalem was noted in Mark 10:32. Jesus knew what lay ahead of Him, and He lovingly prepared His followers for the tragic events which were to take place [10:32-34].

According to Jesus' own prediction, the chief priests, the scribes, and their associates, would be responsible for condemning Him to death [10:33]. Therefore, every mention of their hostile attitude towards Jesus becomes another clue in fixing the blame for His suffering. [In this passage, look particularly at 11:18, 27, 28; 12:12.]

Two questions asked of Jesus give the key word for Mark 11. 'By what authority doest thou these things? and who gave thee this authority to do these things?' [11:28]. As He approached the cross Jesus demonstrated His authority in four different circumstances.

The triumphal entry 11:1-11 *Jesus' authority as King*

Setting: Place..

Jesus' preparations

Instructions to two disciples (*1*) ....

(*2*) .... (*3*) ....

(*4*) ....

Explanation of instructions ....

....

Instructions obeyed by the disciples ....

....

[60]

Instructions obeyed by owner of the colt ....

Jesus' Entry into Jerusalem

The King honoured [8] ....

....

The King praised [9, 10] ....

....

....

The King in the temple [11] ....

The King spending the night in .... with His

...., probably in the home of .... [11]

This entry of Jesus into Jerusalem was a direct fulfilment of the prophecy of Zechariah [Zech 9:9]. The general belief among the Jews was that He should come riding upon an ass. In contrast with the horse, which was a symbol of war, the ass was a symbol of peace and fittingly carried the Prince of Peace as He presented Himself to the multitudes as their King.

Excitement was high in the city crowded with visiting pilgrims at the Passover season. Multitudes quickly joined the procession as it wound its way towards Jerusalem. Catching the spirit of the occasion, the people threw leafy branches and their outer clothing into the pathway of the lowly beast with its royal burden. Shouts of triumph and acclaim rose spontaneously from the people, who quoted Psalm 118:25, 26 implying that they hailed Jesus as their promised Messiah.

Hosanna is the Hebrew word for 'Save now.' Psalm 118:25 was always sung during the procession around the temple altar at the most important feasts. The expression had come to be used like any other shout of acclaim, such as 'God save the Queen!,' but on the occasion of the triumphal entry the people no doubt were thinking of the original meaning of the Messianic Psalm. Of course, the Jews anticipated an earthly kingdom which would free them from the humiliation of the Roman rule. In a few more days the crowds would be calling 'Crucify Him!' when their hopes for the immediate establishment of the kingdom were dashed. Forgetting the shouts and forgiving the cruelty of the multitudes, Jesus rode confidently toward the city which would reject Him and put Him to death.

Jesus not only portrayed His authority as King, but He also exercised His authority as He demanded the use of the colt from its owner.

[61]

Cursing the fig tree 11:12-14 *Jesus' authority as Judge*

Setting: Day........................[probable]   Place ....

Coming from .... early on .... morning of the final week of Jesus' life, Jesus was .... Seeing in the distance a fig tree full of .... He turned towards it, anticipating some fresh .... for breakfast. Disappointed to find no ...., He cursed the tree so that it would never again bear fruit.

This is the only miracle of judgment which Jesus performed. The miracle was also a parable which pictured the nation Israel making a profession of godliness without any heart reality. Fig trees usually bear fruit before the leaves appear. Jesus had every right to expect figs when He saw a fig tree full of leaves. In the same way, He had the right to expect His own people to bear the fruits of righteous living, but their hearts were hardened against Him.

Cleansing the temple 11:15-19 *Jesus' authority as Priest [Messiah]*

Setting: City .... Place ....

On the previous day Jesus had entered the temple [11:11] and had 'looked round about upon all things' there, as one who had full right to inspect the place.

The crowds of Jews who came to Jerusalem from all over the world to observe the Passover provided a rich source of income for the native Jews. Animals for sacrifice were sold by merchants in the temple court to the worshippers who could not supply their own. The coins from all foreign countries were changed by money-changers 'for a price' into the special coinage required by the temple authorities [Exod 30:13].

What was wrong with these temple practices? Jesus did not object to the sale of animals nor to the changing of money. But He did object to the transacting of business [doubtless accompanied by much fraudulent practice] inside the temple court which should have been kept sacred for worship. The animals could have been sold outside the temple area. Money could have been exchanged without a charge for the service. And the temple area never should have been used as a thoroughfare by those wishing to take a short-cut from the market to their homes.

List Jesus' acts in His temple clean-up.

(1) ....

(2) ....

[62]

(3) ....

(4) ....

The authority for Jesus' actions was pictured in two Old Testament prophecies.
[See Isa 56:7 and Jer 7:11] How was that authority expressed? ....

....

....

Was the temple to be a house of prayer for Jews only?.......................................

For whom?.................................... Whom did Jesus mean? ....

Instead of a house of prayer, Jesus called the temple a ....

.... It had become like a cave inhabited by bandits

who disputed and quarrelled over their spoils.

What was the effect of Jesus' acts in the temple upon the scribes and chief priests?

....

....

What was the effect on the people? ....

At the close of a busy day, where did Jesus go? ....

Lesson from the withered fig tree 11:20-26 *Jesus' authority as Teacher*

Setting: Day .... Place [11:12] ....

Peter's perplexity ....

Jesus' reply ....

Jesus gave no further explanation for the cursing of the fig tree on the previous
day, but He did desire to increase the faith of the disciples in the power of God to
perform miracles. These few verses teach a grand lesson on the power of faith.

The power of faith

The object of faith ....

The prayer of faith [23, 24] ....

....

....

A forgiving spirit essential to faith ....

....

Faith is not 'believing something that isn't so'; faith is belief because it knows the power and will of God. Any mountains of sin, of temptation, of opposition, or of suffering may be removed by an act of faith in God who performs miracles.

Jesus' authority challenged 11:27-33

Setting: City .... Place ....

The challengers ....

The double challenge ....

....

Jesus' question put to the challengers ....

....

The challengers' confusion ....

....

....

The result: The challengers *would* not answer Jesus' question; Jesus therefore *would* not answer theirs.

If the challengers had admitted that John's message of repentance came from God, they would have been forced also to admit that Jesus' message and power came from God. They knew the answer, but they tried to appear not to know! Their sin was not ignorance of the truth; it was failure to obey the truth of which at heart they were convinced.

The parable of the wicked husbandmen 12:1-12

Though Jesus did not give His enemies a direct reply concerning His authority, He told them a parable which pointed to the answer.

Here is the story in brief:

A certain man planted a vineyard and rented it out to tenant farmers and went away. At various times he sent to the farmers servants to collect fruit from his vineyard. In turn they were shamefully treated – beaten, stoned, and even killed. Finally he sent his only son, thinking that the farmers would respect him. But they killed him, too, casting him out of the vineyard. Now what would the owner of the vineyard do? He will destroy the tenants and give the vineyard to others.

Rewrite the story substituting 'God' for *A certain man*, 'nation Israel' for *vineyard*, 'religious leaders' for *tenant farmers*, 'prophets' for *servants*, and 'fruit of righteousness' for *fruit*.

....

....

....

....

....

....

....

....

....

....

....

....

....

The chief priests, the scribes, and the elders understood only too well the meaning of the parable, 'for they knew that he [Jesus] had spoken the parable against them' [12]. They recognized the quotation from Psalm 118:22, 'The stone which the builders rejected is become the head of the corner,' which they knew was always applied to their coming Messiah. Yet here was Messiah, and they were rejecting Him.

Jesus' parable brought conviction to the hearts of the Jewish religious leaders, but they were still unrepentant. They left Him for a little while to return when a new opportunity for questions would arise.

REVIEW

Locate on map: Bethphage, Bethany, Mount of Olives.

Jesus demonstrated His authority as King, Judge, Priest, and Teacher. Be able to tell *how* He accomplished His purpose.

Insincerity is a word which well describes the Jewish religious leaders. How did their words and actions [chap. 11] give proof of this insincerity?

What words fittingly describe their attitude toward Jesus, as exhibited in this lesson?

Titles of Jesus	By whom given
11:3	....
11:21	....

12 *A day of questions*

[12:13-14]

The religious leaders of the Jews continued their deliberate plot 'to catch' Jesus 'in his words.' This chapter contains four difficult questions which they hoped Jesus could not answer.

Question about tribute to Caesar 12:13-17

By whom asked? ....

Why asked? ....

Manner of address to Jesus ....

What the questioners thought of Jesus ....

....

Were they sincere? .... Explain your answer.........................

....

The question asked ....

Jesus' knowledge of the questioners ....

Jesus' object lesson

The object ....

Its superscription [around edge of coin]...

Jesus' pronouncement ....

....

If Jesus had answered 'Yes' to the question, the Pharisees would have labelled Him unpatriotic to the Jews. If He said 'No,' the Herodians would report Him as hostile to the Roman government. Jesus' reply revealed that everyone has a responsibility both to government and to God. The answer left the Pharisees and Herodians amazed at His wisdom. [The coin was called a denarius.]

Question about the resurrection 12:18-27

By whom asked? .... Their belief [compare Acts 23:8] ....

.... Manner of address to Jesus ....

The Sadducees' quotation from the law of Moses [Deut. 25:5].........................

....

....

The case stated [probably an imagined situation greatly exaggerated] ....

....

....

....

....

The question asked ....

....

Jesus' reply: The Sadducees were wrong because (1) ....

....

and (2)...

The Sadducees began their questioning with a quotation from the law of Moses, apparently accepting it as truth. Their difficulty was that they failed to believe the *whole* law. Jesus gave them further teaching concerning (1) the fact of the resurrection, and (2) the conditions of the resurrection life.

(1) The fact of the resurrection. Abraham, Isaac, Jacob – and all the rest of the Old Testament saints – are not dead but living. The unfulfilled promises which were given to them during their lifetime will have to be made good at some future time when their bodies have been raised from the dead. So, it is obvious that their spirits live on until they will be reclothed with glorious resurrection bodies. How will this be accomplished? By the power of God! Jesus' resurrection a few days later was a renewed pledge to all believers of their own future resurrection.

(2) The conditions of the resurrection life. Only a few hints about resurrection life are given in the Bible. Jesus gave to the Sadducees, however, a glimpse into the future. All those who rise from the dead will experience a new kind of life. A spiritual body will take the place of the present natural body, and the former human relationships of earth will no longer apply.

[68]

Question about the greatest commandment 12:28-34

By whom asked? ....[Matt 22:34, 35]

The Jews divided the law given in the Pentateuch [first five books of the Old Testament] into 613 precepts, 365 prohibitions [as many as the days of the year], and 248 commandments [as many as the parts of the body]. Some of these were considered greater and some lesser in their importance. Many were the arguments which attempted to settle the question as to which was the greatest of all. 'Among the greater commandments they reckoned Sabbath observance, circumcision, rules of sacrifice and offerings, and rules about fringes and phylacteries' [*Thomas M. Lindsay*].

The question:..

Jesus' answer [in three parts]

(1) [Compare Deut 6:4] ....

(2) [Compare Deut 6:5 and Luke 10:27] ....

....

....

(3) [Compare Lev 19:18] ....

....

Did the scribe agree with Jesus?..

Did he add anything to Jesus' answer? ....

What was it? ....

....

What was Jesus' estimate of His questioner? ....

....

What was the effect on the crowd who heard this discussion?...........

....

Question of Christ concerning His descent from David 12:35-37

The scribes and the Pharisees were silenced by Jesus' answers to their questions which were planned deliberately as a trap. Now Jesus had a question for them to consider.

Setting: Place...

Jesus' question ....

....

The scribes who were always keen students of the Old Testament assented to the belief that Messiah [Christ] would be a descendant of David [Matt 22:42], but this was only part of the truth. Jesus endeavoured to add to their conception of Messiah by quoting David's inspired prediction concerning Him.

What was this prediction? [See also Psalm 110:1] ....

....

....

If David called Messiah his Lord, how could Messiah also be his son? There is only one possible answer. Jesus is both the son of David and the Son of God; He is both human and divine. [Luke 1:30-33.] If the scribes and Pharisees had been willing to accept Jesus for all that He is, their answer would have come quickly and easily. Instead they were silenced once again [Matt 22:46].

What was the reaction of the 'common people'? ....

....

Jesus' warning against the scribes 12:38-40

Those who were the religious teachers of the Jewish religion rejected the true prophet from heaven when He offered Himself to them. Therefore, they deserved the condemnation which Jesus spoke against them. Note three kinds of sins which they committed.

1. The scribes' love for display and show

(1) ....

(2) ....

(3) ....

(4) ....

2. The scribes' greed...

3. The scribes' hypocrisy ....

Jesus' promise of punishment ....

The guilt and punishment of the religious leaders were 'greater' because their responsibility and sin were 'greater'.

[70]

Commendation of the widow's offering 12:41-44

Jesus now moved into the large quadrangle of the temple called 'the Court of the Women.' Here stood the thirteen golden trumpet-shaped chests which received the offerings of the worshippers as they left the temple. This place was known as the treasury.

What was Jesus doing at the place of offering? ....

....

What did He see the rich doing? ....

The poor widow doing? ....

The mite was 'the smallest copper coin in use among the Jews, two of which was the *smallest offering allowed* to be given into the treasury' [*T. M. Lindsay*].

How did Jesus compare the widow's offering with the offerings of the rich people?

....

Why was this true? ....

What is Jesus' standard for giving? ....

....

REVIEW

Look up in a Bible dictionary: Pharisees, Herodians, Sadducees.

Titles of Jesus	By whom given
v 14	....
v 19	....
v 32	....
v 35	....
v 37	....

What three questions did the critics of Jesus ask Him? ....

....

....

[71]

What was the purpose of the questions? ....

....

Did they receive the replies for which they looked? Explain your answer. ....

....

....

What effect did Jesus' replies have upon his questioners? Were they convinced, or not?

How do you know?..

....

Contrast the spirit of the scribes [38-40] with the spirit of the poor widow [41-44].

....

....

....

....

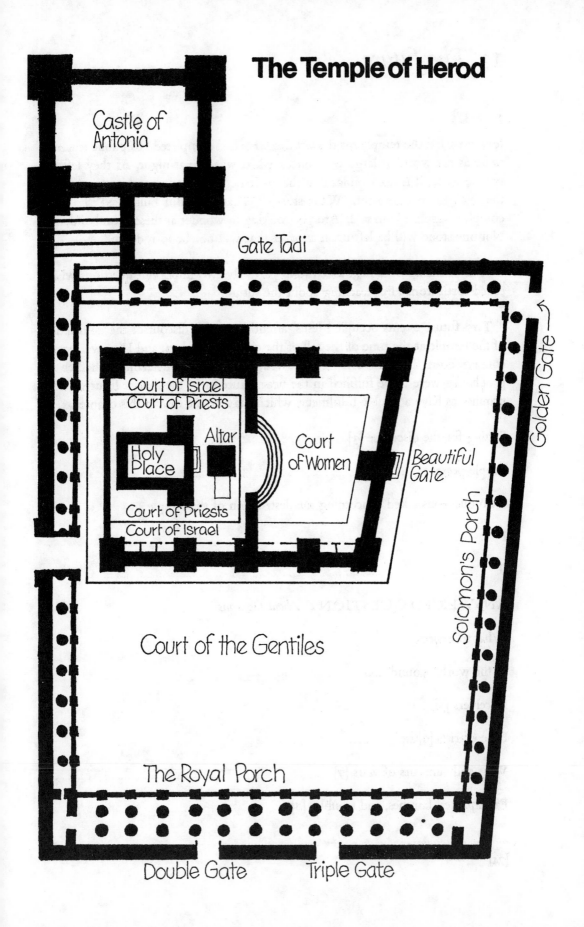

The Temple of Herod

Castle of
Antonia

Gate Tadi

Court of Israel
Court of Priests

Altar

Holy
Place

Court
of Women

Beautiful
Gate

Court of Priests
Court of Israel

Golden Gate →

Solomon's Porch

Court of the Gentiles

The Royal Porch

Double Gate   Triple Gate

13 *The future*

[13:1-37]

Jesus now left the temple for the last time. He had completed His public teaching as far as the world at large was concerned. It was late at night. As they left the temple scene, it is no wonder that the majestic and massive architecture caused the disciples to comment, 'What stones! What beautiful buildings!' To their complete surprise Jesus said, 'Are you looking in wonder at these great buildings? Not one stone will be left upon another that will not be torn down.'

Four of the apostles next asked Jesus privately two important questions which called forth from Him teaching about the future.

Two future events occupied Jesus' attention in this discourse: the destruction of the temple at the time of the fall of the city of Jerusalem, and His own second coming. From the discussion that followed, it is difficult to determine whether the prophecies were to be fulfilled in the near future or in the distant future. Often prophecies have a double fulfilment, which may be the case in this chapter.

Setting for the discourse [3] ....

People present ....

Two questions asked concerning the destruction of the temple

I ....

II ....

ANSWER TO QUESTION II *About the signs*

What to expect

In the world around you

Deceivers [5] ....

False Christs [6] ....

Wars and rumours of wars [7] ....

Earthquakes, famines, and troubles [8] ....

....

As witnesses of the gospel

Imprisonment [9] ....

Beatings [9] ....

Arraignment [9] ....

Betrayal within families [12] ....

....

Hatred [13] ....

The 'abomination of desolation' [14]

This is usually taken to mean the desecration and destruction of the temple. An ancient historian, Josephus [*Wars of the Jews*, IV, 6], refers to an opinion popular in his time that 'Jerusalem would be taken, and the temple be destroyed, when it had been defiled by the hands of the Jews themselves.' This actually occurred when warring factions of the Jews fought for supremacy and the right to defend their city and their temple from the invading Romans. It may be that Jesus looked back to Daniel's prophecy [Dan 9:27] and saw its fulfilment in the strife between the Zealots and the Assassins. These two parties carried their fighting inside the temple where many of them were murdered. This desecration of the temple could have been the defilement 'by the hands of the Jews themselves', referred to by Josephus, which was to precede the capture of Jerusalem and the destruction of the temple. All of the 'troubles' which preceded the destruction of Jerusalem might, in turn, be symbols pointing to the preparation for the second coming of Christ.

What the disciples were to do:

Flee to the mountains [14]

Without delay of entering one's house [15]

Without delay of returning from the field for extra clothing [16]

Hindrances to flight – helpless mothers and dependent children [17]

Pray for flight – that it be not in the winter [18]

General concluding description:

Unparalleled *affliction* [19]

Shortened for the elect's sake [20]

Unparalleled *deception* [21, 22]

False Christs and false prophets

Signs and wonders

ANSWER TO QUESTION I *About the time*

To find the answer to the disciples' question, 'When shall these things be . . .?' compare Mark 13:14 with Luke 21:20, 21. Note the relationship in the parallel columns below.

MARK 13:14	LUKE 21:20, 21a
But when ye shall see the abomination of desolation, spoken of by Daniel the prophet, . . . then let them that be in Judaea flee to the mountains . . .	And when ye shall see Jerusalem compassed with armies, then know that the desolation thereof is nigh. Then let them which are in Judaea flee to the mountains . . .

Jesus' predictions recorded by the two Gospel writers fit together to give the complete picture. Wars, famine, and persecution would precede the end, but the presence of enemy armies outside the city walls would be the final signal for the complete destruction of the temple and the city. This was fulfilled in 70 A.D., about 40 years after the crucifixion of Christ.

The prediction of Christ's second coming 13:24-27

ANSWER TO QUESTION II *About the signs*

The signs in the heavens which will precede His coming [24, 25]

....

....

....

....

The appearance of the Son of Man [26]

Where? ....

How? ....

The gathering of the elect [27]

By whom?...

[76]

From where? ....

....

The pledge of Christ's coming again 13:28-31

The reliability of nature [shown in the parable of the fig tree, 28, 29]

....

....

The reliability of God's Word [30, 31] ....

....

....

['This generation': Sometimes, in Scripture, the word 'generation' does not mean the people living during a period of 30 or 40 years but during an indefinite age-long period. See, for example, Psalm 22:30; 24:6; Acts 2:40.]

ANSWER TO QUESTION I   *About the time*

'After that tribulation' [24]

This phrase marks a transition of Jesus' discourse from the destruction of the temple and the city of Jerusalem to His own return to earth. In God's time programme 'One day is . . . as a thousand years, and a thousand years as one day' [2 Pet 3:8]. Nineteen centuries have now passed since the destruction of Jerusalem; and more years, it may be, will come and go before the glorious hope of Christ's return shall be fulfilled.

Only the Father knows the time ....

....

.... [32]

The challenge of Christ's coming again 13:32-37

There are three challenges to Christians as they wait for Christ's return.

What are they? [33] ....   [Beware] ....

....

In other words, always be ready, for 'ye know not ....

....

Tell the parable of the porter [34-37] as a modern story.

[Jesus took His story from the work of the priests, whose duty it was to see that the night guards of the temple faithfully kept their watches. No one knew when the 'captain of the temple' would make his rounds – whether at even [6 to 9 P.M.], or at midnight [9 to 12 P.M.], or at cockcrowing [12 P.M. to 3 A.M.], or in the morning [3 A.M. to 6 A.M.]. If a guard was found asleep on duty, he was punished by a severe beating or by having his clothes set on fire.]

....

....

....

....

....

....

....

There are two aspects of 'watching.' The command, 'Watch,' could mean, 'Be alert,' or 'Don't go to sleep.' Both need to be emphasized.

Three don'ts for the followers of Jesus

(Consult the whole chapter.)

(1) Don't be deceived by ....

....

(2) Don't be troubled by ....

....

(3) Don't worry beforehand about your defence before rulers. ....

....

....

Three do's for the followers of Jesus

(Consult the whole chapter.)

(1) Preach the gospel ....

[78]

(2) Speak in the power of the Holy Spirit ....

....

(3) Endure to the end ....

REVIEW

To be sure of the fact of Christ's coming again, study these references in the order given: John 14:3; Acts 1:9b-11; Mark 13:26, 31.

To learn the tragic details of the desecration of the temple and destruction of Jerusalem in 70 A.D., read Josephus' account of the destruction of Jerusalem. Does the historian's description match the predictions of Jesus? Find the parallels. It is said that many Christians escaped the torture in 70 A.D. by obeying Jesus' warnings given on the Mount of Olives before His death [Mark 13 and parallel passages].

Remember that as Jesus previewed the actual overthrow of Jerusalem by Roman armies, He used the description of that historical event to portray His own coming again.

Titles of Jesus	By whom given
v 1	....
v 26	....
v 34	....

14 *Facing death*

[14:1-72]

The Passover was the greatest religious and national festival of the Jews, commemorating their deliverance from Egypt [Exod 12]. The feast of unleavened bread was considered a part of the Passover feast. It could only be celebrated in Jerusalem, and was the occasion for the visit of vast crowds of pilgrims. It always came in the spring.

Plot against Jesus' life 14:1, 2

The time..

The plotters ....

Objective of the plot ....

Why was action delayed? ....

....

Jesus facing death with His friends 14:3-9

This episode may have taken place on the evening of the preceding Saturday, the Jewish Sabbath [John 12:2-8] but was inserted at this point by Mark to connect the story with the treachery of Judas.

Setting: City .... Home ....

Occasion...

A woman's gift...

....

Its presentation to Jesus ....

....

Objections ....

....

Jesus' evaluation of the gift ....

Value of the gift to Jesus ....

....

Reward to the woman for her gift ....

....

[Read the same incident told from John's viewpoint, John 12:1-9.]

Identify the *woman* ...., and the *objector* to the gift ....

The plot by the traitor 14:10, 11

Name of the traitor ....

With whom did he identify himself? ....

The plot ....

....

The offer accepted ....

The bargain ....

Traitor on the 'look-out' ....

....

Facing death with the disciples 14:12-32

Preparations for the Passover 12-16

Time ....

Jesus' instructions to two disciples

Find a man ....

Find a home ....

Find a guest room ....

Make ready ....

Instructions obeyed ....

....

The Passover was observed in the time of Jesus somewhat in the following way. On the table were two or three flat cakes or thin biscuits of unleavened bread [Exod 12:18], and four cups of red wine mixed with water before the master of the feast.

(1) He took one of the cups, called the *cup of consecration*, 'gave thanks,' tasted the cup, and passed it around.

(2) Water was then brought in; first the master and then the others washed.

(3) The table was next set with bitter herbs (lettuce, endive, beet, etc) and a sauce called *charoseth* (made of dates, raisins, figs, and vinegar, pounded and mixed together), and the paschal lamb (Latin 'paschalis' = passover).

(4) After thanksgiving the master took a portion of the bitter herbs, about 'the size of an olive,' and dipping it in the sauce ate it, as did the others.

(5) The second cup of wine was filled, and then followed the *haggadah* or showing forth [1 Cor 11:26]. A child or a proselyte (convert to Judaism) asked, 'What mean ye by this service?' [Exod 12:26] and the master of the feast answered at great length. The first part of the *Hallel* [Psa 113-114) was sung and the second cup was solemnly passed around.

(6) The master again washed his hands, and taking two of the cakes of unleavened bread, broke them, gave thanks, and distributed them to the company, each of whom took a piece, dipped it in the sauce and ate it. Some authorities say that if any *stranger* was present he was given a portion, but had no other share in the meal. This sheds light on Jesus' giving the sop to Judas.

(7) The paschal lamb was next eaten.

(8) After thanksgiving the third cup or *cup of blessing* [1 Cor 10:16] was passed round.

(9) Thanks were given for the food received; the fourth cup, the *cup of joy*, was handed around. Then followed the singing of the second part of the *Hallel* [Psa 115-118] and the company separated.

The Passover Meal 17-21

Time of day .... Those present..

....

Announcement of the traitor ....

Questions of the disciples..

Identification of the traitor ....

....

Condemnation of the traitor ....

....

The Last Supper 22-25

It is not known whether or not Jesus and His disciples followed all nine of the
procedures usually connected with the celebration of the Passover. [Putting
together the four Gospel accounts, five of the nine may be identified: (1), (2), (4),
(5), and (6).] Against a background of offerings and blood sacrifices, however,
Jesus gave His disciples a picture of a new relationship with them – He was the
Paschal Lamb whose death would do away with the necessity for any further
offerings.

Jesus took bread and ....

....

....

Jesus took the cup and ....

....

....

Jesus' prediction concerning Himself ....

....

....

The bread and the wine were substituted for the usual Passover foods and were
used to represent the body and blood of Christ soon to be sacrificed on the cross.
Thus, a new Covenant [agreement] was established between God and His people
and no other sacrifice would ever need to be offered again.

The Last Supper, or the Lord's Supper for Christians today, not only looks back
to the final perfect sacrifice for sin, but ahead to Christ's new kingdom where His
children will reside forever [25].

On the Mount of Olives 26-31

Jesus' warning to the disciples...

....

....

[To be offended means to be *made to stumble*. See the prophecy in Zech 13:7.]

Explain 'smitten shepherd' ....

.............................and 'scattered sheep' ....

Jesus' prediction concerning Himself..

....

Peter's loyalty ....

Jesus' prediction concerning Peter ....

....

Peter's boast ....

....

How did the rest of the apostles feel? ....

....

Facing death in Gethsemane 14:32-42

Companions of Jesus...

The test of Jesus in Gethsemane

Pick out four phrases that help to describe Jesus' sorrow ....

....

....

Jesus' request of His disciples ....

....

Jesus' petition of His Father..

....

Jesus' resignation to the Father's will..

....

The testing of the disciples in Gethsemane

What were they asked to do?.. ....

....

What actually did they do?...

How many times was their failure repeated? ....

What was the reason for their failure? ....

The arrival of the traitor

Jesus' action ....

Facing death with the traitor 14:42-45

The traitor

His name .... His associates ....

His companions on this occasion ....

Sent by whom?..

How armed? ....

His prearranged signal ....

His address to Jesus ....

His act of betrayal...

The arrest

How accomplished?...

A friend's quick defence ....

[See John 18:10] Who was this 'friend'? ....

Jesus' question of His captors ....

....

Why did they not need 'arms'?...

....

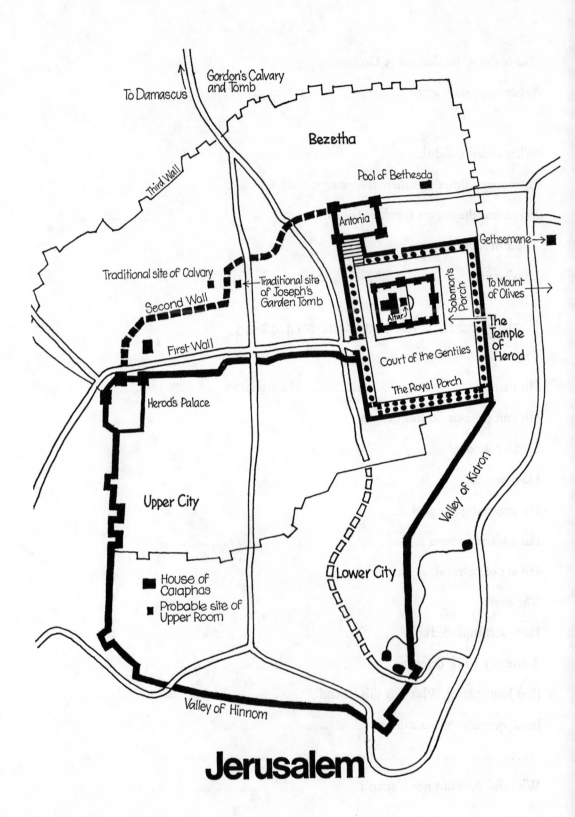

To Damascus

Gordon's Calvary
and Tomb

Bezetha

Third Wall

Pool of Bethesda

Antonia

Gethsemane

Traditional site of Calvary

Traditional site
of Joseph's
Garden Tomb

Second Wall

Solomon's Porch

To Mount
of Olives

Altar

First Wall

The
Temple
of
Herod

Court of the Gentiles

Herod's Palace

The Royal Porch

Valley of Kidron

Upper City

Lower City

■ House of
Caiaphas
■ Probable site of
Upper Room

Valley of Hinnom

Jerusalem

Jesus forsaken

Disciples? ....

'Certain young man' ....

....

[Only Mark mentions this 'certain young man.' Could he have been the author
of this Gospel? Some think that he was. If so, this is the only hint of the author in
the Gospel attributed to him.]

Facing death before the high priest 14:53-65

This was the trial before the Jewish religious authorities – the high priest and the
Sanhedrin.

The judge .... The jury..

....

Disciples present ....

[See also John 18:15, 16]

Legal witnesses sought – with what success? ....

False witnesses called

One of Jesus' claims misrepresented ....

....

Lack of agreement ....

Cross-examination by the high priest

The high priest's question ....

....

Jesus' answer ....

The high priest's second question ....

....

Jesus' answer ....

....

The high priest's dramatic action ....

Verdict ....

Sentence ....

Jesus mocked by the Jews ....

....

....

Failure of Peter 14:66-72

The dialogue presented here is like a short scene in a drama. Arrange the setting and action around the questions and answers.

Setting for the episode: Place ....

Maid: [setting ....]

....

Peter: ....

Cock's signal ....

Maid: [setting ....]

....

Peter: ....

Bystanders: ....

Peter: [action ....]

....

Cock's signal ....

Peter's memory refreshed ....

Peter's emotions touched ....

REVIEW

Locate on map of city of Jerusalem: Gethsemane, Upper Room, palace [John 18:13], temple, Mount of Olives. Trace each change of location in this chapter with its accompanying event.

Identify: Simon the leper, Judas Iscariot, Peter; Peter, James and John as a unit.

Write a short biographical sketch of Peter as he appears in this chapter. Take note of his boastfulness, lack of watchfulness, timidity, etc.

Compare the two suppers in this chapter: 3-9 and 22-25. Mention the hosts, guests, purpose of the meal, etc.

Titles of Jesus	By whom given
v 14	....
v 21	....
v 45	....
v 61	....
v 61	....
v 67	....

List each use of the title *Son of man* in this chapter. To whom does it refer? By whom is it always used?

15 Crucifixion
[15:1-47]

Early the next morning, after a quick consultation, Jesus was transferred from the Jewish religious authorities to Pontius Pilate [see Luke 3:1], the Roman governor of Judaea. In Jewish law the Sanhedrin had the power to inflict the sentence of death, but under Roman rule such a sentence had to be confirmed by the governor.

The trial before Pilate 15:1-20

Pilate's question of Jesus ....

Jesus' answer ....

Accusations of the chief priests ....

Jesus' defence..

Pilate's alternative offered to the Jews ....

....

....

....

Offer accepted or rejected? ....

Demand of the mob..

Sentence passed by Pilate..

....

What insults did Jesus suffer before He was taken out to be crucified? ....

....

....

....

....

The crucifixion 15:21-38

The circumstances of the crucifixion 21-28

Place ....

Who helped Jesus reach the place of crucifixion? ....

.... What did he do? ....

A drink offered [to dull pain] ....

Accepted or not? ....

Careless and hardened soldiers ....

....

Superscription [title] on Jesus' cross ....

....

Two other crosses...

Fulfilment of Scripture [Isa 53:12] ....

....

The ridicule flung at Jesus 29-32

The title on the cross ....

The taunts of the passers-by ....

....

....

....

The mockery of the chief priests ....

....

....

....

The abuse of the thieves ....

The last three hours [noon to 3 P.M.] 33-38

Darkness over the land..

Jesus' last prayer to His Father ....

....

Mistaken by whom?..

Mistaken for what? ....

....

Jesus' voluntary surrender of life ....

The rent veil in the temple ....

[This heavy curtain separated from men's view the Holy of Holies where God's presence dwelt. When sin was put away by the death of Christ, the Holiest place could be entered directly 'by a new and living way,' God's Son, Heb 10:19, 20.]

Witnesses of Jesus' death 15:39-41

Centurion ....

....

Devoted women ....

....

....

From where?..

The burial 15:42-47

Time .... Day...

Request of Joseph of Arimathaea (probably a few miles north of Jerusalem) ....

....

Pilate's surprise ....

Centurion's testimony to Jesus' death ....

Joseph's request granted ....
[92]

Getting ready for burial ....

....

Place of burial ....

Witnesses of burial ....

REVIEW

Locate on map of city of Jerusalem: Herod's Palace [which Pilate occupied when he visited Jerusalem], Golgotha [traditional site is the Church of the Holy Sepulchre; however, many think that Gordon's Calvary – close to the Damascus Gate – with its nearby garden tomb is a more satisfactory answer to the problem of the exact location].

Locate on map of Palestine: Magdala.

Retell the story of this chapter, centring your ideas around the following people: Pilate, Barabbas, Simon the Cyrenian, the centurion, the women, Joseph of Arimathaea.

Titles of Jesus	By whom given
v 2	....
v 9	....
v 12	....
v 18	....
v 26	....
v 32	....
v 32	....
v 39	....

Compare the trial before the high priest and the trial before Pilate in the following chart [14:53-65, 15:1-20].

	The religious trial	The civil trial
Judge		
Jury		

	The religious trial	The civil trial
Time		
Accusers		
Accusations		
Witnesses		
Silences of Jesus		
Testimony of Jesus		
Attitude of judge		
Mockery		
Cruelties		
Verdict		

16 Resurrection

[16:1-20]

The only break between the last verse of the fifteenth chapter and the first verse of the sixteenth chapter was the observance of the Sabbath. The burial of Jesus had been rushed because of the approach of the Sabbath which began on the evening of the day of the crucifixion. On the next evening – after the Sabbath ended – more spices to complete the burial were purchased. Then, early the next morning the women came to finish their task. Apparently they had completely forgotten Jesus' predictions that He would rise again, or, which is more probable, they had not understood them.

The resurrection 16:1-8

Setting: Day ....

Time .... Place ....

The women ....

....

Their difficulty ....

....

Their surprise...

Their fear ....

....

The 'young man' [angel, Matt 28:5]

His place...

His clothing ....

His message ....

....

His command ....

....

Effect of the message upon the women ....

....

Jesus' appearances after the resurrection 16:9-14

To Mary Magdalene..

Her mission ....

....

Effect of the news...

To 'two of them' [16:12-13; compare Luke 24:13-35]

Their mission...

Effect of the news ....

To 'the eleven'

Jesus upbraided [found fault with] them because.................................

....

....

The great commission 16:15-19

(1) Go ....

(2) Preach ....

(3) Baptize ....

(4) Signs and miracles ....

....

[96]

The ascension 16:19

(1) ....

(2) ....

The commission obeyed 16:20

(1) ....

(2) ....

(3) ....

(4) ....

REVIEW

What evidences for Jesus' resurrection does Mark present to his readers?

Can you account for the fear and unbelief which gripped all of Jesus' followers?

Titles of Jesus	By whom given
v 6	....
v 19	....
v 20	....

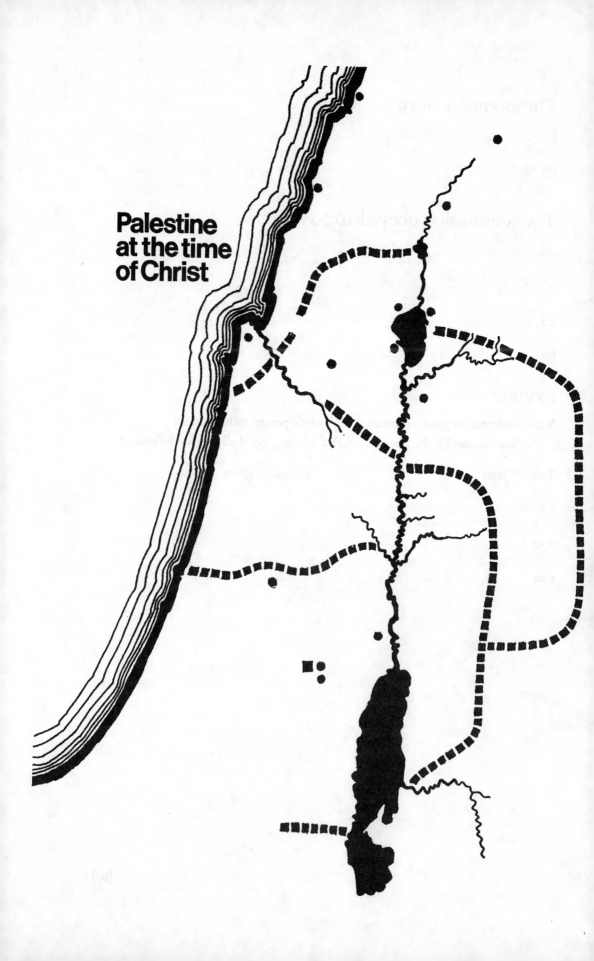

**Palestine
at the time
of Christ**

Tips for teachers

The workbook technique is widely recognized and accepted as a medium for learning various skills. Too often, however, the method calls only for selection from multiple choice, true or false designations, or finding a five-letter word beginning with 'g'. The present workbook is so planned that its users will go direct to the Bible for all the answers. Instead of endless disconnected words and phrases which seem to have no apparent relation with one another, the answers will fit into an outline of Mark's story of Christ. Thus, when the workbook is complete, the skeleton outline will be padded with 'meat,' and will furnish a satisfying account of Jesus' ministry on earth. The aim throughout its preparation has been to provide a modified inductive study of the Gospel of Mark.

There are some portions of the study which need more explanation than answer-hunting. Consult chapter 2 for an example. Review questions at the close of this chapter will integrate the content under discussion.

This workbook is not a commentary on Mark and therefore cannot anticipate all the questions which might be raised. Neither can it give on each point explanations that a Bible dictionary might provide. Some simple explanations or definitions have been included *in loco* and in the glossary, but the teacher should implement the information contained herein.

The primary aim of this study is to stress facts rather than interpretation. The interpretation of events and the personal application of the teaching are left in the hands of the teacher who will use the workbook as a self-starter for personal Bible study.

Mark's sketchbook of Christ may be used as a short course to be covered in three or four weeks as in a summer camping programme, or for once-a-week religious instruction. On the other hand, it may be expanded into a long-term course in schools by using the suggestions offered at the close of each chapter. Research projects could include looking up topics in Bible dictionaries – geographical sites, biographical sketches, customs in Palestine, etc. Frequent drills will aid the student in retaining the facts of the life of Christ. The possibilities are unlimited.

Two maps of Palestine are included for good reason. One [in the frontispiece] includes all places mentioned in Mark's Gospel. The second may be used for review since it indicates locations without naming them.

For the simplest form of analysis, chapter divisions [with few exceptions] are followed. Two brief outlines listed on page 101 may help to organize the chapters into a logical sequence. Perhaps the teacher will be anxious to produce his own outline of the Gospel. Try it!

[99]

This study, though prepared with teen-agers in mind, should prove useful for all young Christians just beginning serious Bible study.

Each teacher should first complete the entire study before trying to teach others. A Bible dictionary and atlas, and one or two reliable translations of the New Testament other than the Authorized Version will be helpful.

In all your teaching let Mark, who was divinely inspired to record his story, present Jesus Christ as the busy Servant who came 'to minister,' and as the Son of God who gave 'his life a ransom for many' [10:45].

Outlines of the Gospel of Mark

Presentation of the person 1:1-13

Demonstration of power 1:14-5:43
  Miracles
  Authority of teaching

Reactions of people 6:1-10:52
  Multitudes
  Disciples
  Pharisees
  Peter
  Various individuals

Declaration of purpose
  [8:32, 9:32, 10:32-34]

Completion of passion 11:1-15:47

Fulfilment of promises 16:1-20
  Resurrection

The preparation   1:1-13

Year of popularity in Galilee 1:14-6:30

Year of opposition 6:30-10:52
  Ministry in Galilee }
  Journeys of flight } 6:30-9:50
  Peraea 10:1-31
  Judaea 10:32-52

Events of passion week 11:1-15:47
  First day of the week 11:1-11
  Monday 11:12-19
  Tuesday 11:20-13:37
  Wednesday 14:1, 2, 10, 11
    [*Jesus in quiet, Judas in Jerusalem*]
  Thursday 14:12-52
  Friday 14:53-15:47
  Sabbath [*Christ in the tomb*] 16:1

Resurrection and ascension 16:1-20
  Appearances
  Commission

Special projects

At the close of each chapter in the study of Mark, there are questions suggested for REVIEW. In some cases insufficient space is left for the answers. For these and other topics you may use the extra pages at the back of the workbook, or plan for a supplementary notebook.

Make a list of all the titles ascribed to Jesus, noting by whom they were given. Which titles refer to His humanity, and which to His deity? What do these many titles teach about Jesus' life and work?

List the 18 miracles and the 7 parables found in Mark, each with its appropriate reference.

Mark's story pushes along swiftly by use of the words 'straightway,' 'immediately,' 'anon,' 'forthwith,' and 'as soon as', forty times. These words are translations of one word in the original Greek language. See how many of the words you can find. What is their significance?

Various reactions to Jesus are carefully noted by Mark. Read through the entire Gospel looking for reactions of amazement, astonishment, fear, hostility, hatred, controversy, love, loyalty, etc. What event or teaching produced each reaction?

Glossary

Centurion: A Roman soldier in charge of one hundred men.

Chief priests: The ruling high priest, other high priests who had preceded him in office, and members of their families.

Chief priests, scribes, and elders: When mentioned as a group they are taken to mean the Sanhedrin; a clique which kept plotting Jesus' death [8:31; 10:33; 11:18; etc].

Corban: Designates money, goods, or services dedicated to God, usually to avoid using them for the sake of dependent needy parents.

Disciples of John: That is, of John the Baptist.

Herod: Herod Antipas, son of Herod the Great, reigning king of Galilee and Peraea.

Herodians: A party of influential Jews supporting the rule of Herod, who united with the Pharisees [their natural enemies] to plot against Jesus.

High priest: The highest officer in Judaism, appointed and removed at will by the Roman ruler; at Jesus' trial, Caiaphas [Mark 14:53; John 18:24].

Law, or *law of Moses:* Usually taken to mean the Pentateuch [first five books of the Old Testament].

Passover: The chief feast of the Jewish religious year; first celebrated in Egypt when the death angel passed over the homes which were protected by the blood sprinkled on the door posts; celebrated each year as a reminder of God's deliverance of His people from the bondage of Egypt [Exodus 12:3-42].

Pharisees: The strictest sect of Jews, who prided themselves on carefully keeping the law of Moses, and all the traditions that had grown up around the law; believed in a future life and lived morally upright lives; denounced by Jesus as self-righteous hypocrites who paid closer attention to minute details of the traditions than to the main spirit of the law.

Pilate: Roman governor of Judaea; to foster his popularity with the Jews, he allowed Jesus to be condemned to death.

Ruler of synagogue: Chief officer of the synagogue who presided over its services, and appointed those who took part in them [Acts 13:15], and was responsible for correct behaviour [Luke 13:14].

Sabbath: The seventh day of the week which was the official day of rest and worship for the Jews.

Sadducees: A sect of Jews, bitter opponents of the Pharisees, who kept the law but not the traditions of the elders; did not believe in a future life; teamed up with the Pharisees to oppose and plot against Jesus [see Acts 23:8].

Sanhedrin: The highest official council or court of the Jews, composed of 70 men, presided over by the high priest; had the power of life and death, though the verdict had to be confirmed by the Roman authorities; had its own police to make arrests [Mark 14:43]; condemned Jesus [Mark 14:64].

Scribes: Were Jews who were students and teachers of the law [originally, copyists of the law, tracing their profession back to Ezra the priestly scribe, Ezra 7:6, 10]; many conducted their own schools, exercising considerable influence on the religious thought of their time.

Scrip: A leather bag or wallet made from an animal skin, slung over the shoulder for carrying provisions.

Synagogue: The local Jewish place of worship which also served as law court and community school; no sacrifices offered, but they were places for reading and explaining 'the law and the prophets' – that is, the Old Testament Scriptures; members of the congregation were sometimes asked to take part in the services [Luke 4:16-22].

Temple: Temple of Jesus' day built during reign of Herod the Great; centre of national life of the Jews; sacrifices and ritual of their religion prescribed by the Old Testament carried on there.

Traditions of the elders: The unwritten law which God supposedly delivered orally to Moses, who, in turn, delivered it orally to the elders; comments and interpretations of the law by various scribes which became a part of the 'traditions'; in Jesus' day, the traditions more binding than the original law of Moses.

Notes